Bake Breads from Frozen Dough

by Sylvia Ogren

DILLON PRESS, INC. / Minneapolis, Minnesota

Dillon Press, Inc., 500 South Third Street
Minneapolis, Minnesota 55415

Printed in the United States of America

Library of Congress Cataloging in Publication Data

Ogren, Sylvia.
  Bake breads from frozen dough.
  1. Bread. 2. Dough. I. Title.
  Includes index.
TX 769.037   641.8'15   76-25064
ISBN 0-87518-137-6

ON THE COVER:
1. *Luncheon Bubble Ring with Shrimp Salad*
2. *Oatmeal Wheat Bread*
3. *Moravian Coffee Cake*
4. *Frosty Snowball Cakes*
5. *Butter Crust Vienna Bread*
6. *Streusel Nut Squares*
7. *White Mountain Loaf*
8. *Butter Crumb Rolls*
9. *Double-Quick Dinner Rolls*
10. *Cinnamon Buns*
11. *Apple Pastries*

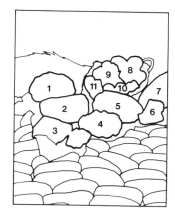

Contents

Introduction 4

For the Beginner 6

Special Know-How for Baking with Frozen Doughs 8

Thawing Frozen Dough in Microwave 12

Bread Loaves 13

Dinner Rolls 30

Sweet Rolls 43

Coffee Cakes 64

Ethnic Breads 85

Supper and Snack Breads 97

Breads Men Like to Bake 110

Appendix
    Recipes to Enhance Breads 118
    Good to the Last Crumb 121
    Decorative Decoupage Bread Wreath 123

Index 124

Introduction

As we think back, one of our fondest memories is the good food that used to come from our mother's and grandmother's kitchens. I grew up on a farm where there was always an abundant supply of good food. One of the things I fondly remember is homebaked bread every Wednesday and Saturday. On Wednesday my mother usually made the basic loaves of bread that we loved to smother with fresh creamery butter and homemade jams and jellies. Saturday was very special because it meant delicious Swedish rye bread. Also on that day, part of the white bread was made into cinnamon rolls, rich and gooey on the bottom, and those great sandwich or dinner buns no one else but my mother could make. One of my secret desires was to bake bread that was just as good as my mother's. Perhaps I have achieved that goal, but even if I haven't, one of the things I really enjoy baking is bread. There's a special satisfaction that comes from baking bread.

Times have changed! Bread baking is no longer a necessity, and, as a result, many people have never taken the time to learn how to make bread. Now, when you would really like a loaf of homemade bread, you may be just a little afraid to tackle baking from scratch—perhaps that little packet of yeast frightens you, or you're not quite sure just how much flour to add, how to knead, how long to knead, or how long to let the dough rise. For others, a busy schedule just doesn't seem to leave enough time to bake bread.

Frozen bread doughs have made it possible for everyone, yes everyone, to make bread, and you're going to love it. Golden, plump, crusty loaves of all shapes and sizes fresh from the oven add a sparkle to the eye and joy to the heart. And they are sure to win praises from the family. Time is no longer a problem. In fact, after baking with frozen dough a few times, you'll know just how much time it takes and you will be able to set the bread out to thaw and rise and be ready to bake at a time that fits your schedule. A perfect loaf of bread is always assured; those little skills necessary for baking a loaf of bread have been done for you. But you can still enjoy the aroma of bread baking.

Another great thing about frozen doughs is that many, many dinner rolls, coffee cakes, and sweet rolls can be made from them. This book has more than three hundred recipe ideas that start with a frozen loaf of dough.

Don't overlook the importance of bread in the daily diet. It is a necessity. Bread has always had an important role in good nutrition. The breaking of bread and its part in mankind's struggle for survival date back farther than Biblical days. Bread and cereals make up one of the four basic food groups. Four or more servings are recommended daily for a good balanced diet. Enriched breads and cereals are important sources of riboflavin, niacin, thiamine, and iron. They also provide us with carbohydrates, starches, and sugars, which give us the quick energy necessary to start the day. A sandwich with a glass of milk is an excellent, inexpensive source of good protein. In this day of rising prices, bread still remains one of the most economical foods—so let's remember to plan to serve it in the daily menu.

One of my purposes in developing and writing this cookbook was to share with you some of the fun that I have had in baking bread. As you look through the book, you will find extremely easy, but fun, recipes to start with. After baking with frozen doughs for a while, you will want to try some of the more special recipes, such as Danish Pastry.

So, happy baking!

For the Beginner

Are you a first-time baker? Or have you thought of baking bread but never quite had the courage? With frozen bread dough you can relax and enjoy bread baking. Forget about how warm to get the water for softening the yeast, how to mix, and how to knead. All these steps have been done for you. And just the right proportion of ingredients has been combined to make perfect bread every time. You can have the fun of reshaping, if desired, watching the bread rise, and then enjoying the aroma of bread baking. The greatest thrill of all is serving homebaked breads.

Before you start baking, read the Know-How section of this book. And read the tips at the beginning of the other sections. It's also important to read the directions and tips on the label of the bread dough you are using.

Below are two lists that give easy variations to start you baking. To begin, you can do something as simple as placing the loaf of frozen dough on a greased cookie sheet, brushing it with beaten egg, and sprinkling it with sesame seed. No shaping whatsoever, yet a crunchy, unique loaf of bread that takes on a real homemade look. When you've made a few things on the first list, try the second list, which is for the advanced beginner. These recipes include simple shaping ideas. Once you've tried a number of these recipes, you'll be ready to bake any recipe in this book.

FOR THE BEGINNER

Bundt Bread, page 17
Butter Crumb Rolls, page 34
Butter Crust Vienna Bread, page 20
Casserole Herb Bread, page 17
Cinnamon Buns, page 44
Cookie Buns, page 57
Double-Quick Dinner Rolls, page 38

Luncheon Bubble Ring, page 100
Moravian Coffee Cake, page 85
Oatmeal Wheat Bread, page 115
Pan Bread, page 17
Sally Lunn, page 87
Skillet Beef-Burger, page 104
Streusel Coffee Cake, page 75
Swedish Tosca Coffee Cake, page 76

Dutch Sugar Cake, page 75
Hamburger Hearth Buns, page 40
Hearth Bread, page 15

White Mountain Loaf, page 112
White Mountain Rolls, page 33

FOR THE ADVANCED BEGINNER

Apple Pastries, page 60
Beef Bake, page 103
Blueberry Flip, page 78
Bubble Dinner Bread, page 16.
Butter Crumb Monkey Loaf,
   page 21
Butterscotch Bubble Loaf,
   page 78
Butterscotch Snowballs, page 72
Can Bread, page 21
Doughnut Chips, page 114
Easy Danish Kuchen, page 71

Frosty Snowball Cakes, page 73
Grecian Feast Bread, page 91
Half 'n Half Bread, page 27
Individual Loaves, page 24
Lemon Drops, page 59
Monkey Bread, page 69
Parker House Loaf, page 18
Patio Cheese Snacks, page 117
Skillet Bread, page 18
Steak Sandwich Loaf, page 113
Streusel Nut Squares, page 55

Special Know·How for Frozen Dough

Starting right is important in all baking and cooking. Below are a few tips to remember about frozen doughs. If you treat the product right, you can be assured of beautiful breads.

Buy a good product. When purchasing frozen dough at the supermarket, be selective.

• Be sure that the product is frozen solid and that the loaves have a good shape. Misshapen loaves could mean the product has been thawed and has lost some of its yeast action. The dough should have a clean creamy white color; if the dough is gray, that is a good indication that the product is old or has been mishandled and has lost much yeast action.

• The package should be free of holes. Excess air will cause the dough to dry out or to get what is sometimes referred to as freezer burn.

• Another indication of an old or poor product is a package that is full of ice crystals.

Store frozen loaves carefully. Keep the dough frozen. Do not freeze it again after it has thawed. Every time the dough thaws, some yeast action is lost, which means that the bread will rise less or take longer to rise when you want to bake it.

• If the dough should thaw, it is better to let it rise and bake it right away. Then you can freeze the baked bread.

• If there is to be a long delay between your trip to the supermarket and your arrival home, keep the bread dough wrapped in an insulated bag.

• Frozen doughs should be stored in the home freezer no longer than a month or two. If you can't use the product within this time, bake it and then freeze it. Be sure the dough is in a place in the freezer where it will remain solidly frozen. The door shelf is not a good place. Keep it in a refrigerator freezer no more than a month. When taking a loaf from a package, *hurry* it back to the freezer. To close the opened package, press out excess air, twist top tightly, and seal with wire twists. A well-closed package helps retain freshness.

Use good baking techniques. To make a basic loaf of bread, follow the directions on the label. For delicious variations, use one of the recipes in this book. No matter how you use your bread dough, you should read the tips and suggestions that follow.

• Read the recipe before you start baking. Be sure you have all the ingredients.

• Use standard measuring cups and spoons for recipes in this book.

• Temperature is one of the most important factors in determining the length of time needed for the dough to rise. In fact, with frozen dough you can control the time needed for rising by controlling the temperature, and then you can have the product ready to bake at a time that fits your schedule. If the temperature is about 90° F., a loaf can thaw and rise and be ready to bake in four hours or less. At a temperature of 70° F., you can expect the bread to take about six hours to rise.

• If you want, set a frozen loaf in the refrigerator in the morning or the night before and let it thaw and rise in the pan. Take it out of the refrigerator to rise a couple of hours before baking time. Time needed for the dough to rise after removal from the refrigerator will depend on how long (and how cold) it has been in the refrigerator. I have stored dough in the refrigerator for two or three days. It is still useable, but I have found that it makes a better product if reshaped into a loaf or used for dinner rolls or sweet rolls.

• Warm places to let dough rise:
in front of a sunny window
near a steady flow of warm air
on top of a range warmed by a pilot light

• If you have an electric oven, here is a good rising method to use: Place a pan of boiling water on the bottom shelf. Set the pan of bread dough on the shelf above the water. (Do not turn on oven heat.) Reheat water one or two times while bread is rising. Do not cover the bread dough, because the steam keeps it moist. Ten minutes before baking, take out the risen bread and preheat the oven. This method takes three to four hours. If this method is used in an oven with a pilot light, keep the oven door open about two inches.

• Here's another fast way to let dough thaw and rise: Heat the oven to 200° F. Then turn off the heat (this is very important) and put the frozen dough in the oven. Place a pan of boiling water in the oven to keep the top moist. With a gas oven, keep the door ajar about two inches so the bread won't get too warm from the pilot light.

• Cover bread loosely with plastic wrap or slip it into a large plastic bag when it is rising. Be sure to allow space for the dough to rise. Making a tent cover with aluminum foil works well too. If the bread is not covered, it could form a crust on the top and not rise well.

• Let frozen bread dough rise before rolling it out for the recipes in this book. Frozen dough is much easier to roll out and use if it has risen to at least double in size. Do a minimum of handling in transferring the risen dough to the rolling surface. Do not knead or shape into a ball. If kneaded or reshaped, the gluten will tighten and it will be more difficult to roll out and shape the loaf. Place the risen dough on a floured surface and start rolling out and stretching to the desired size. Lift the dough and reflour the surface lightly. You may even want to turn the dough over while rolling. Do not flour the surface too heavily. Let the dough adhere very slightly to the surface here and there along the edge.

• Use a soft brush for spreading butter or egg white on bread dough. (A good one is a soft paint brush about one inch wide.) A soft brush is especially important if the shaped dough has risen before brushing.

• *Always* preheat the oven to the recommended temperature before placing the bread in the oven.

• When it has finished baking, bread should have a rich golden brown color and sound hollow when you tap it.

• Always remove breads from the pan immediately after baking. If bread is left in or on the pan, it will form soggy crust.

• Many breads are best if they have a fresh warm taste. This does not mean last-minute baking. To reheat, wrap in foil and heat in a 350° F. oven about fifteen minutes just before serving. If the bread is frozen, it will take at least thirty minutes to reheat. A microwave oven takes only seconds to reheat bread. The bread should not be wrapped in foil for the microwave oven; follow the directions included with your oven.

• To store baked breads, first let them cool completely. Then place in a tight bread storage container or a plastic bag. Refrigerator storage generally hastens drying and should be used only if the weather is hot and humid or if the bread is to be kept several days.

• Save energy by preparing and baking several loaves of frozen bread dough at the same time. Make the standard bread as well as variations from this book. Freeze the extra bread to serve later. This will save time as well as energy, and it will be convenient to have some bread all prepared and ready to serve. It's impressive to be able to take a loaf of homemade bread from the freezer and serve it in a moment's notice.

Freeze bread carefully: Baked yeast breads freeze very well. If good freezing techniques are used, the frozen product will be as light and tender as the product was when placed in the freezer. Freezing does not improve a product, but it will maintain its original quality. Three months is the recommended maximum length of time for storing breads in the freezer. Below are tips important to freezing baked breads.

• Wrap for freezing as soon as *completely* cooled. Do not let bread get dry or stale before freezing.

• Cut or package in meal-size amounts.

• Good packaging is important to maintain the quality. Select a wrapping material that is moisture-proof, strong, and durable. A good quality plastic bag works very well, or use heavy-duty foil. If foil is used, the bread can be reheated in the oven in the freezer wrap.

• In wrapping, exclude as much air as possible. Air left in the package will cause drying or freezer burn. (Holes or tears in the packaging material will also cause drying of the frozen products.)

• Seal tightly.

• Label and date the package before freezing. Masking tape works well for foil-wrapped packages. A label can be tucked inside plastic bags before sealing.

• Thaw breads in the original wrap; unwrap just before serving. Thawing at room temperature will take about one to three hours, depending on the size of the product and warmth of the room. For a warm product, thaw in a 350° F. oven. This will take about fifteen to thirty minutes, depending on size of product. Wrap in foil for heating in the oven.

• Frozen breads require only minutes to thaw and heat in a microwave oven. Check your microwave oven manual for specific information on heating breads. Most ovens recommend placing unwrapped breads on a paper plate and laying a paper towel across the top before heating. Use the defrost cycle to thaw the bread.

Thawing Frozen Dough in Microwave

- Place 1 to 1½ cups hot water in a flat dish larger than your bread loaf pan. Be sure to use only glass or microwave-proof dishes. Grease the bread pan heavily, and butter the frozen loaf of dough on all sides. Put the loaf in the bread pan and set in the dish of water in the microwave oven.
- Microwave at half power (50 percent, medium, or defrost for most ovens) 4 minutes. Turn the dish holding the water ¼ turn every minute. After the first 2 minutes, turn the dough over and cover the ends with small pieces of foil. Let it stand in the oven 10 minutes. Continue to microwave, 1 minute at a time, until the dough is thawed and slightly warm, turning after each minute.
- If the oven has 30 percent power, microwave 6 minutes, turning every 1½ minutes and covering ends of dough after 3 minutes. With 10 percent power, microwave 15 minutes, turning every 5 minutes and covering ends after 10 minutes.
- After thawing, reshape the dough into a loaf as described for an old-fashioned loaf, page 15, or cover and let rise until doubled in size. Then shape, let rise, and bake as directed in recipe.

HOW TO LET DOUGH RISE IN THE MICROWAVE

- You may use this method with dough that is rising before it is to be shaped and with dough that has already been shaped. Be sure to use only glass or microwave-proof dishes. If the dough has been shaped, the pan must be one that can also be used in a conventional oven.
- Place the thawed dough in a greased loaf pan or dish. Set it in a larger pan that contains 1 to 1½ cups hot water, and lay a piece of waxed paper on top.
- Microwave at half power (50 percent, medium, or defrost for most ovens) 1 minute. Let it stand in the oven 10 minutes. Turn the dish holding the water ¼ turn and repeat the process until the dough has doubled in size or is 1 inch above the sides of the pan.
- If your oven has 30 percent power, microwave 1½ minutes and let stand 10 minutes. Continue process until doubled in size. With 10 percent power, microwave 5 minutes and let stand 10 minutes. Lower powers are better to use because there is less chance for parts of the loaf to get too hot.
- Bake in a conventional oven for a nicely browned product.

Bread Loaves

How exciting! The aroma of homemade bread streaming from the kitchen and a golden plump loaf to bring warm to the dinner table. Yes, this can be you, and you can say, "I baked it!"

If you have never baked a loaf of bread from frozen dough, don't wait any longer. In this section you'll find round loaves, flat loaves, long loaves, squatty loaves, and high light loaves. You'll find loaves embraced with a butter-rich crust or snuggled under a crackling toasty coating—ones that look like bread baked on a hearth or in Grandma's wood range. Grandma probably spent hours making the bread, and you can do it with so little effort!

A loaf of bread is the easiest way to start. Select something as easy as White Mountain Loaf. Just brush the loaf with lots of soft butter and roll it in flour; place it on a cookie sheet and let it rise and spread casually. You'll be thrilled with the old-fashioned look. For a round shape try Pan Bread, or make the long French-Style Bread. Next perhaps you'll make the Butter Crumb Monkey Loaf, with its crunchy herb coating of buttery bread crumbs—so easy but oh, so good! After a little experimentation with these simple shapes, you're going to want to try Mix and Match Bread, using two kinds of bread dough.

Baking helps for dinner loaves:

• The preferred pan for the basic loaf is the $8\frac{1}{2} \times 4\frac{1}{2} \times 2\frac{1}{2}$-inch pan. However, the $9\frac{5}{8} \times 5\frac{1}{2} \times 2\frac{3}{4}$-inch pan makes a nice loaf too. It is not as high, but it is good for sandwiches and toasting. (In the recipes in this book these two pans will be referred to as the 8x4- or 9x5-inch pans.) If smaller pans are used, the risen loaf may bulge over the sides and even collapse in the center. The $10\frac{1}{4} \times 3\frac{5}{8} \times 2\frac{5}{8}$-inch pan makes a well-shaped longer loaf. It is especially nice for open-faced sandwiches.

• For a loaf that is well-browned all the way around, use dull-finished metal or glass baking pan.

• If the pan is new, place it in a 375° F. oven about one hour.

• The bread pan should be well greased on the sides as well as the bottom. The loaf will brown better and not stick. A butter wrapper will not grease the pan well enough. You should be able to see the streaks of shortening.

• The baked loaf should have a deep golden color all the way around. The loaf will sound hollow when thumped with the knuckles or fingers. If underbaked, the loaf may collapse. If overbaked, it may shrink before it is removed from the oven.

• Remove baked bread from pan immediately; this prevents a soggy crust.

• Cool bread on a wire rack. Many kinds of loaves retain a better shape if placed on their sides to cool.

• For a shiny, crisp crust, brush the loaf with an Egg Wash before letting it rise or just before baking. An Egg Wash is a mixture of equal amounts of slightly beaten egg or egg white and water. If 1 teaspoon water to 1 tablespoon egg is used, the crust will be even shinier.

• For a soft shiny crust, brush the baked loaf with soft or melted butter.

• Use a serrated knife for slicing bread. Put the loaf on its side and cut back and forth with a good sawing motion. An electric knife also works well for slicing bread.

• Store baked bread in a tight bread storage container or plastic bag. Refrigerator storage generally hastens drying and should be used only if bread is to be kept several days or if the weather is hot and humid.

• Bread freezes very well, and if it will not be used in several days keep it fresh by freezing part of it.

• Homebaked bread makes great toast. For convenience, slice bread when cold, then place it in a plastic bag and freeze. The frozen slices can be popped into the toaster.

• Rising temperature and the age of the bread dough determine how long it is going to take to rise. The important point is to let it rise until it appears light in texture and more than doubled in size. In bread loaf pans it is easy to tell when it has risen enough. In the 8x4-inch pan, it will be a good inch above the sides of the pan. In the 9x5-inch pan, it will be about three-quarters to one inch above the sides.

• Most of the variations in this section call for white bread dough. In many of the recipes another flavor could be used. Use your own discretion as to whether or not you would like the flavor combination with another kind of bread. White and honey wheat bread doughs are most readily available in all parts of the country. Some of the more special flavors of bread dough, such as sweet or French, may not be marketed in your area.

Quick Tricks with a loaf of bread:

• It's so easy and adds a personal touch and a homemade flavor: brush the frozen or partially thawed loaf of bread with melted butter and sprinkle with one of these salts—seasoned, garlic, or onion—or just brush the loaf with one of the flavored butters on page 120. For a sweet touch, brush the loaf with the butter and sprinkle with a flavored sugar, page 121; decrease the baking temperature to 350° F.

• Another easy idea is to brush the frozen loaf with an Egg Wash, page 121, and sprinkle with crushed herbs. Or brush the loaf with Egg Wash and then sprinkle with sesame, poppy, or other seed.

An old-fashioned loaf:

• The package labels have complete directions for the simplest method of baking a loaf of standard bread. Some cooks think they add a bit more of the old-fashioned texture of homemade bread by using this technique: Let the dough thaw and rise in a large plastic bag until it appears light and almost doubled in size. Roll it out on a floured surface to a 14x7-inch rectangle and roll it up, starting with a 7-inch side. Seal bottom seam and ends. Place in well-greased bread pan. Let it rise until about 1 inch above sides of pan, 45 to 60 minutes. Bake as directed. The texture will be finer and more like an old-fashioned loaf of bread. The volume will be higher. I especially like this method with honey wheat bread. This method of shaping is good to use if the frozen dough has been in your freezer for several months.

HEARTH BREAD

A special crusty bread—looks just like the loaf of bread baked on Grandmother's wood range, but so much easier.

BAKE: 375° F. for 30 to 35 minutes   MAKES: 1 loaf

1 tablespoon egg
1 teaspoon water
1 loaf frozen white (honey wheat or French) bread dough
sesame seed
corn meal

Combine egg with water; brush top half of frozen loaf with mixture and sprinkle generously with sesame seed. Place on greased cookie sheet sprinkled with corn meal. Cover; let rise in warm place until very light or doubled in size. (A frozen loaf will take from 3 to 6 hours to rise, depending on rising temperature.)

Bake at 375° F. for 30 to 35 minutes.

BUBBLE DINNER BREAD

*Bubbles of bread are coated wtih cheese. Serve it warm,
and each person can pull off a bubble. Slice loaf when served
cold.*

BAKE: 375° F. for 30 to 35 minutes   MAKES: 1 loaf

1 loaf frozen white bread dough, thawed
¼ cup butter or margarine, melted
½ cup grated Parmesan cheese

Divide dough into 24 pieces. Using fork, coat each piece with butter,
then cheese. Place bubbles in well-greased 9x5-inch pan, a bundt pan,
or a 2-quart casserole. Cover; let rise in warm place until very light or
doubled in size, 1½ to 2 hours.

Bake at 375° F. for 30 to 35 minutes, or until deep golden brown. Remove
from pan immediately.

NOTE: Herb butter, page 120, may be used if desired; omit cheese.

FRENCH-LIKE BREAD

*A loaf of frozen bread dough takes on a French look. To serve,
cut diagonally into thick slices, brush with butter, wrap in foil,
and heat in 350° F. oven 10 to 15 minutes.*

BAKE: 375° F. for 25 to 30 minutes   MAKES: 1 loaf

1 loaf frozen white bread dough, thawed
1 tablespoon egg white
1 teaspoon water
sesame seed or poppy seed, if desired

Let dough rise until almost doubled in size. Roll out on floured surface
to a 15x7-inch rectangle. Roll up, starting with 15-inch side. Place
diagonally on well-greased cookie sheet. Brush with egg white mixed
with water; sprinkle with seed. Make 5 or 6 cuts across the top. Cover;
let rise in warm place until very light or doubled in size, 1 to 1½ hours.
Bake at 375° F. for 25 to 30 minutes.

SERVING SUGGESTIONS:

FRENCH BREAD TOASTS: Melt ½ cup *butter* or margarine (season with herbs
or garlic, if desired). Cut bread into 1-inch slices. Brush both sides with butter.
Just before serving, toast both sides on grill over hot charcoal, or under **broiler.**

BARBECUE BEEF LOAF: Split loaf in half horizontally. Combine 1 pound lean
ground beef , 1cup (8 oz.) *tomato sauce*, ⅓ cup chopped *onion*, 1 cup shredded
Cheddar or American *cheese*, ½ teaspoon each: *sugar, salt,* and *chili powder.*
Spread mixture over bread halves. Place each on cookie sheet. Bake open-faced
at 375° F. for 30 to 35 minutes. Makes 6 to 8 servings.

PAN BREAD

It's easy to make and fun to serve. Take the loaf of bread to the table on a bread board and let each person slice off a chunk of warm bread. Great with steak or hamburger!

BAKE: 375° F. for 30 to 35 minutes   MAKES: 1 round loaf

1 loaf frozen bread dough (white, honey wheat, French, or other flavor), thawed

Shape thawed dough into a round loaf (or divide in half for two small loaves); place in greased 9-inch round pan. Cover; let rise in warm place until light or doubled in size, 1½ to 2 hours.

Bake at 375° F. for 30 to 35 minutes.

Quick Trick: Brush top with an equal amount of egg or egg white and water; sprinkle with sesame seed, if desired. Make several shallow cuts across the top to make an X or a checkerboard pattern.

BUNDT BREAD

Bread baked in a bundt pan is as light and tender as angel food cake.

BAKE: 375° F. for 30 to 35 minutes   MAKES: 1 bundt loaf

1 loaf frozen white (honey wheat or French) bread dough, thawed

Shape dough into a 12-inch strip. Form into a ring; seal ends together. Place in well-greased 9- or 12-cup bundt pan. Cover; let rise in warm place until light or doubled in size, 1½ to 2 hours.

Bake at 375° F. for 30 to 35 minutes. (If bundt pan is heavy cast aluminum, decrease baking temperature to 350° F.)

CASSEROLE HERB BREAD

The buttery crust is aromatic with herbs. Bring the bread to the table on a bread board and let each person cut off a slice. Delicious warm.

BAKE: 375° F. for 35 to 40 minutes   MAKES: 1 loaf

2 tablespoons butter or margarine, soft or melted
1 teaspoon mixed herbs (oregano, thyme, marjoram, parsley, or others)
1 loaf frozen white bread dough

Combine butter and herbs. Brush entire loaf (preferably frozen) with the butter mixture. Place in well-greased 1½- or 2-quart oval casserole. Cover; let rise as directed on the label.

Bake at 375° F. for 35 to 40 minutes.

PARKER HOUSE LOAF

The dough is flipped over to give the loaf the shape of a giant Parker House roll. The garlic butter gives it a flavor ideal to serve with a steak dinner.

BAKE: 375° F. for 25 to 30 minutes   MAKES: 1 loaf

1 loaf frozen white bread dough, thawed
2 tablespoons butter or margarine, soft or melted
¼ teaspoon garlic powder*

Let dough rise slightly. Combine butter and garlic. Roll out dough to 14x8-inch rectangle on floured surface. Brush with half the garlic butter. Lift 14-inch side and fold to within ½ inch of opposite side. Place on greased cookie sheet. Brush with remaining butter. Cover; let rise in warm place until very light or doubled in size, 1 to 1½ hours.

Bake at 375° F. for 25 to 30 minutes, or until a rich golden brown.

*For a real fresh garlic flavor, use ½ garlic clove, mashed and chopped.

SKILLET BREAD

Bacon and onion enhance a loaf of supper bread.

BAKE: 350° F. for 25 to 30 minutes   MAKES: 1 round loaf

1 loaf frozen white bread dough, thawed
2 slices bacon, cut in small pieces
½ cup chopped onion.

In 9- or 10-inch skillet, fry bacon until partially cooked. Sprinkle with onion; *do not cook.* Shape dough into ball; flatten to about 1 inch. Place in skillet. Cover; let rise in warm place until light or doubled in size, 1½ to 2 hours.

Bake at 350° F. for 25 to 30 minutes. Turn out of skillet immediately. Best warm.

Bread Loaves:
1. Checkered Loaf
2. Parker House Loaf
3. Butter Crumb Monkey Loaf
4. Lebanese Bread
5. Hearth Bread
6. Triple Treat Bread
7. Golden Crown
8. Cheese Bubble Loaf
9. Snack Wheat Bread
10. French Herb Bread
11. Steak Sandwich Bread
12. Honey Bee Twist

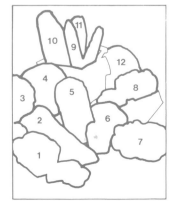

BUTTER CRUST VIENNA BREAD

Butter seeps into the crust to make bread extra light and give it a country fresh flavor.

BAKE: 375° F. for 30 to 35 minutes   MAKES: 1 loaf

1 loaf frozen white (or French) bread dough, thawed
2 tablespoons butter or margarine

Place loaf on greased cookie sheet. Make a cut with sharp knife, ½-inch deep, lengthwise down center of loaf. Cut butter into thin slices and place in cut. Cover; let rise in warm place until very light and more than doubled in size, 1 to 1½ hours.

Bake at 375° F. for 30 to 35 minutes. Brush with more butter, if desired.

RAISIN BREAD

Always a favorite with the youngsters—it makes great toast.

BAKE: 375° F. for 30 to 35 minutes   MAKES: 1 loaf

1 loaf frozen white (or honey wheat) bread dough, thawed
½ to 1 cup raisins

Let dough rise slightly; then flatten to ½ inch. Sprinkle with raisins; fold in half. Roll out to a 14x7-inch rectangle. Roll up, starting with 7-inch side. Place in well-greased 8x4- or 9x5-inch pan. Cover; let rise in warm place until about 1 inch above sides of pan, 1½ to 2 hours.

Bake at 375° F. for 30 to 35 minutes.

SUGGESTION: After placing dough in pan, brush with melted butter and sprinkle with cinnamon sugar.

HONEY BEE TWIST

Honey butter and a twist of nutmeg enhance this twisted loaf of breakfast or coffee bread.

BAKE: 350° F. for 30 to 35 minutes   MAKES: 1 round loaf

1 loaf frozen white (or honey wheat) bread dough, thawed
2 tablespoons soft butter or margarine
2 tablespoons honey
⅛ teaspoon nutmeg

Let dough rise until almost doubled in size. Shape into a 24-inch strip on floured surface. Starting in center and keeping dough flat, coil into a well-greased 9-inch round pan or on a cookie sheet, lined with foil. Combine butter, honey, and nutmeg; brush over dough. Cover; let rise in warm place until light or doubled in size, 45 to 60 minutes.

Bake at 350° F. for 30 to 35 minutes. Remove from pan immediately.

CAN BREAD

Perfectly shaped round slices are great for open-faced sand-wiches. You'll like the hint of lemon in these slices.

BAKE: 350° F. for 25 to 30 minutes   MAKES: 3 small tall loaves

1 loaf frozen white (honey wheat or French) bread dough, thawed
1 ½ tablespoons soft butter or margarine
1 teaspoon grated lemon peel, if desired

Divide dough into thirds; shape into balls. Combine butter and peel; butter three 1-pound coffee cans (or 30-oz. fruit cans) generously. Place balls of dough in cans. Cover; let rise in warm place until light or doubled in size, 1½ to 2 hours.

Bake at 350° F. for 25 to 30 minutes. Remove from cans immediately.

OTHER CAN SIZES TO USE:
Divide dough in half and use two 2-lb. coffee cans or 3-lb. shortening cans. Or divide dough into fourths and use four 1-lb. shortening cans or 1-lb. fruit and vegetable cans.

NOTE: If the dough has started to rise when divided and shaped, it may not need the 1½-hour rising time.

BUTTER CRUMB MONKEY LOAF

Toasty crumbs enhance the bubbles of bread. It's such an easy way to make a great loaf of bread.

BAKE: 375° F. for 30 to 35 minutes   MAKES: 1 loaf

1 loaf frozen white bread dough, thawed
½ cup bread crumbs
1 teaspoon dried chives or parsley
¼ teaspoon each: oregano, thyme, marjoram, basil
¼ cup butter or margarine, melted

Divide dough into 24 pieces. Combine crumbs and herbs. Coat pieces of dough with butter, then crumbs. Layer in greased 9x5-inch pan. Cover; let rise in warm place until it almost fills the pan, 1½ to 2 hours.

Bake at 375° F. for 30 to 35 minutes. Carefully remove from pan. Good warm.

TIP: A 2-quart casserole or bundt pan may be used for baking the bread. Crushed soda crackers, corn flakes and other ready-to-eat cereals can be substituted for the bread crumbs.

GOLDEN CROWN

This twisted crown is so pretty you will want to cut it at the dinner table.

BAKE: 375° F. for 25 to 30 minutes   MAKES: 1 large ring

1 loaf frozen white (or honey wheat) bread dough, thawed
1 tablespoon egg or egg white
1 teaspoon water

Let dough rise until doubled in size. Divide in half. Shape each half into a 24-inch strip. Twist the two strips together. Place on greased cookie sheet in a ring, sealing ends together. Combine egg and water; brush on bread. Cover; let rise in warm place until light or doubled in size, 30 to 60 minutes.

Bake at 375° F. for 25 to 30 minutes.

TIP: For an added touch, insert about 15 blanched whole almonds into twist before baking.

HERB LOAF

The easy method below may be used to distribute or incorporate ingredients into a loaf of frozen bread dough to achieve a new flavor in the bread. With bulkier ingredients such as raisins, use ½ to 1 cup. With aromatic herbs, use 1 to 2 teaspoons, and with seeds and peels, about 2 tablespoons.

BAKE: 375° F. for 30 to 35 minutes   MAKES: 1 loaf

1 loaf frozen white (honey wheat or French) bread dough, thawed
¼ teaspoon thyme
¼ teaspoon oregano
¼ teaspoon marjoram
1 teaspoon parsley
1 teaspoon chives

Let dough rise until almost doubled in size. Roll out to a 15x7-inch rectangle. Sprinkle with herbs. Fold in half. Roll out again. Roll up, starting with 7-inch side, sealing with heels of hands. Seal ends. Place in well-greased 8x4 or 9x5-inch pan. Cover; let rise in warm place until about 1 inch above the sides of the pan, about 1 hour.

Bake at 375° F. for 30 to 35 minutes.

FRENCH HERB LOAF:
After adding herbs to dough, roll out to 12x7-inch rectangle. Roll up, starting with 12-inch side. Place on greased cookie sheet. Brush with *egg-water* mixture; sprinkle with more *herbs*. With sharp knife, make 4 or 5 cuts across top. Let rise and bake 25 to 30 minutes. For a crustier loaf, turn oven off and leave bread in oven 10 minutes.

CHEESE NUGGET BREAD

Hot from the oven, the slices of bread taste just like a grilled cheese sandwich.

BAKE: 375° F. for 30 to 35 minutes   MAKES: 1 loaf

1 loaf frozen white (or honey wheat) bread dough, thawed
1 cup (½-inch) Cheddar cheese cubes

Let dough rise slightly. Line a 9-inch round or 9x5-inch pan with 12-inch sheet of foil, allowing edges to remain above sides of pan. Grease well. Flatten dough to about ½ inch. Press cheese cubes into dough. Shape into a round or long loaf. Place in prepared pan. (Be sure all cheese cubes are covered with dough.) Cover; let rise in warm place until light or doubled in size, 1 to 1½ hours.

Bake at 375° F. for 30 to 35 minutes. Remove from pan immediately.

BRAIDED BREAD

Braiding always gives an interesting shape to a loaf of bread.

BAKE: 375° F. for 30 to 35 minutes   MAKES: 1 loaf

1 loaf frozen white (or honey wheat) bread dough, thawed

Let dough rise until almost doubled in size. Divide into thirds. Shape each piece into a 9-inch strip; braid together. Place in well-greased 8x4- or 9x5-inch pan. Cover; let rise in warm place until about 1 inch above top of pan, 1 to 1½ hours.

Bake at 375° F. for 30 to 35 minutes, or until a rich golden brown.

TIP: Loaf may be brushed with an equal amount of egg and water, then sprinkled with poppy or sesame seed.

BUTTERFLAKE LOAF

A unique shape for a loaf of dinner bread. Let guests pull off their own buttered flakes or slices of bread.

BAKE: 375° F. for 20 to 25 minutes   MAKES: 2 small loaves

1 loaf frozen white bread dough, thawed
2 tablespoons butter or margarine, melted
garlic powder or herbs, if desired

Let dough rise until doubled in size. Roll out on floured surface to a 16x12-inch rectangle. Brush with butter; then sprinkle with garlic powder or herbs. Cut into 4x2-inch rectangles. Place half the rectangles, 4-inch side down, in a greased 8x4- or 9x5-inch pan. Repeat with remaining dough. Cover; let rise in warm place until very light, 30 to 45 minutes.

Bake at 375° F. for 20 to 25 minutes, or until a rich golden brown. Serve warm. (Bread may be baked early and wrapped in foil and reheated.)

CINNAMON SWIRL BREAD

Always a favorite for toasting, or try one of the other suggested swirls for something different.

BAKE: 375° F. for 30 to 35 minutes　　　　　　　MAKES: 1 loaf

1 loaf frozen white bread dough, thawed
2 tablespoons sugar
1 ½ teaspoons cinnamon
½ cup raisins, if desired

Let dough rise slightly. Roll out on floured surface to a 15x7-inch rectangle. Sprinkle with a mixture of the sugar, cinnamon, and raisins; press down firmly. Roll up tightly, starting with 7-inch side and sealing after each turn. Place in well-greased 8x4- or 9x5-inch pan. Cover; let rise in warm place until about 1 inch above the sides of pan, 1 to 1½ hours.

Bake at 375° F. for 30 to 35 minutes.

SWIRL VARIATIONS:

Omit the cinnamon, sugar, and raisins, and substitute one of the ideas below:

CHEESE SWIRL: 1 cup shredded *Cheddar cheese* and 1 teaspoon *poppy seed*

ONION SWIRL: ½ cup chopped *green onions* (including tops), 1 teaspoon *caraway seeds,* and a sprinkle of *seasoned salt*

HERB SWIRL: 1 ½ teaspoons mixed *herbs* (oregano, parsley, marjoram, thyme, etc.)

BACON-CHEESE SWIRL: ½ cup crumbled fried *bacon* and ½ cup shredded *Cheddar cheese*

ORANGE RAISIN SWIRL: ¾ cup *raisins* or currants and 1 tablespoon grated *orange peel*

PEANUT BUTTER SWIRL: ½ cup *peanut butter*

HINT: When making pinwheel or swirl loaves, it is important to avoid or eliminate air spaces while rolling up. Roll tightly and press out air bubbles that may form.

INDIVIDUAL LOAVES

A loaf of bread for each person. If you don't have small loaf pans, make loaves round and bake in 5-inch foil pie pans.

BAKE: 375° F. for 20 to 25 minutes　　　　　　MAKES: 6 small loaves

1 loaf frozen white (or honey wheat) bread dough, thawed

Divide dough into 6 parts. Shape into small loaves. Place in well-greased 4½ x 2½ -inch pans. Cover; let rise in warm place until very light or doubled in size, 1 to 1½ hours.

Bake at 375° F. for 20 to 25 minutes.

SCANDINAVIAN WHEAT BREAD

This bread combines two of the favorite flavors of the Scandinavian countries—anise and orange.

BAKE: 375° F. for 30 to 35 minutes   MAKES: 2 small loaves

1 loaf frozen honey wheat bread dough, thawed
2 tablespoons grated orange peel or chopped candied orange peel
1 tablespoon anise or fennel seed

Flatten dough to ½ inch. Sprinkle with peel and seed. Divide in half. Shape into round or oblong loaves. Place on greased cookie sheet. Cut a couple gashes across top with sharp knife. Cover; let rise in warm place until light or doubled in size, 1½ to 2 hours.

Bake at 375° F. for 30 to 35 minutes.

CARAWAY WHEAT BREAD:
Substitute 1 tablespoon *caraway seed* for the orange peel and anise seed.

LEBANESE BREAD

Another ethnic bread. These round crusty loaves are about an inch high when baked. They are fun to serve with a dinner, or make them American with your favorite sandwich filling.

BAKE: 400° F. for 15 to 20 minutes   MAKES: 3 round flat loaves

1 loaf frozen white (honey wheat or French) bread dough, thawed

Let dough rise until doubled in size. Divide into thirds. Roll out each to a 9-inch circle (¼ inch thick) on floured surface. Place on greased cookie sheets. Cover; let rise in warm place until doubled in size, 30 to 60 minutes.

Bake at 400° F. for 15 to 20 minutes. Brush hot loaves with soft butter.

TIP: If desired, brush loaves with egg white and sprinkle with sesame seed before baking.

SANDWICH IDEAS:
Slice Lebanese bread in half horizontally and fill. For a warm sandwich, wrap in foil and heat in 350° F. oven about 15 minutes. To serve, cut into quarters. Use any of these fillings:
    corned beef, sauerkraut, Swiss cheese
    boiled ham, cheese, lettuce
    bacon, lettuce, tomatoes
    chicken, tuna, or egg salad
    sloppy Joe ground beef filling
    taco filling, chopped tomato, lettuce, and shredded cheese
    poor boy filling—luncheon meats, cheeses, pickles, onion, lettuce
    sliced bologna, lettuce, potato salad
    hot broiled frankfurters, sliced, hot pork and beans (Coney Island)
    hot charcoal-broiled top round or flank steak cut across the grain into thin
      slices

CHRISTMAS BREAD

A loaf of bread filled with Christmas goodies is fun for the holiday season. Use it for coffee parties or try it for breakfast toast.

BAKE: 350° F. for 30 to 35 minutes   MAKES: 1 loaf

1 loaf frozen white (or sweet) bread dough, thawed
½ cup mixed candied fruit
¼ cup chopped or sliced almonds
soft butter or margarine
2 tablespoons sugar
½ teaspoon cinnamon

Let dough rise until almost doubled in size. Roll out on floured surface to a 14x7-inch rectangle. Sprinkle half with fruit and almonds. Fold uncovered dough over fruit; roll out again. Roll up, starting with 7-inch side, sealing with heels of hands. Seal ends. Place in well-greased 8x4- or 9x5-inch pan. Brush top with butter. Sprinkle with mixture of the cinnamon and sugar. Cover; let rise in warm place until about 1 inch above sides of pan, 1 to 1½ hours.

Bake at 350° F. for 30 to 35 minutes.

SUGGESTION: Make this bread into 6 miniature loaves (see page 24) and use as special favor gifts.

TRIPLE TREAT LOAF

Three small loaves, each with a different flavor, baked in the same pan. Nice for a small family, when you want one loaf for a meal; the others can be frozen for another time.

BAKE: 375° F. for 30 to 35 minutes   MAKES: 3 small loaves

1 loaf frozen honey wheat bread dough, thawed
¼ cup raisins
1 teaspoon grated orange peel
1 teaspoon caraway seed
1 teaspoon anise seed

Divide dough into 3 parts. Flatten one part and sprinkle with raisins and peel; fold over and shape into small loaf, distributing fruit. Place crosswise in 8x4- or 9x5-inch well-greased pan. Work caraway into one part and anise into the other. Shape into small loaves. Place in same pan. Cover; let rise in warm place until about 1 inch above sides of pan, 1 to 1½ hours.

Bake at 375° F. for 30 to 35 minutes. To serve, separate into small loaves.

MIX AND MATCH BREAD
(Two-Tone Swirl)

White and honey wheat doughs are shaped together to give a variety of patterns in each slice of bread.

BAKE: 375° F. for 30 to 35 minutes MAKES: 2 loaves

1 loaf frozen white bread dough, thawed
1 loaf frozen honey wheat bread dough, thawed

Let dough rise until almost doubled in size. Divide each loaf in half. Roll out one part from each loaf to a 15x7-inch rectangle. Place white dough on top of honey wheat dough. Roll up tightly, sealing with heels of hands. Seal ends. Place seam-side down in well-greased 8x4- or 9x5-inch pan. Repeat with remaining dough. Cover; let rise in warm place until about 1 inch above sides of pans, 1 to 1½ hours.

Bake at 375° F. for 30 to 35 minutes.

MORE MIX AND MATCH IDEAS:

BRAIDS: Divide each loaf into thirds. Shape into 9-inch strips. Braid 3 strips together. Place in well-greased pans. (Or shape into 15-inch strips and place braids on greased cookie sheets.)

PATCHWORK BREAD: Divide each loaf into 20 pieces. Shape into balls. **Place 20 balls in each pan, alternating white and honey wheat.**

HALF 'N HALF BREAD: Divide each loaf in half. Shape into 8-inch strips. Place a white and honey wheat strip side by side in each pan.

CHECKERED LOAF: Divide each loaf into fourths. Shape into 8-inch strips. Place a white and honey wheat strip in each pan. Top each with a second strip, alternating flavors.

CRAZY QUILT ROUND: Divide each loaf in half. Mold together a piece of white and honey wheat dough to make one round loaf. Place on greased cookie sheets or 9-inch round pans.

ORANGE RAISIN WHEAT BREAD

Orange flavor complements the raisins in this whole wheat bread.

BAKE: 350° F. for 30 to 35 minutes MAKES: 1 loaf

1 loaf frozen honey wheat bread dough, thawed
½ cup raisins or currants
1 tablespoon grated orange peel

Let dough rise slightly. Roll out on floured surface to a 14x7-inch rectangle. Sprinkle with raisins and peel; press firmly into dough. Roll up, starting with 7-inch side, sealing with heels of hand while rolling up. Seal ends. Place in well-greased 8x4- or 9x5-inch pan. Cover; let rise in warm place until about 1 inch above sides of pan, 1 to 1½ hours.

Bake at 350° F. for 30 to 35 minutes.

ORANGE PRUNE BREAD

To give an interesting touch to fruit breads, brush loaf after shaping with soft or melted butter, and then sprinkle with cinnamon sugar.

BAKE: 350° F. for 30 to 35 minutes   MAKES: 1 loaf

1 loaf frozen honey wheat bread dough, thawed
1 cup uncooked soft prunes, cut in small pieces
2 teaspoons grated orange peel

Let dough rise until almost doubled in size. Roll out on floured surface to 14x7-inch rectangle. Sprinkle with half the prunes and peel; press down firmly. Fold in half; turn one quarter way around and roll out again. Sprinkle with remaining prunes and peel. Roll up, starting with 7-inch side, sealing with heels of hands after each turn. Seal ends. Place in well-greased 8x4- or 9x5-inch pan. Cover; let rise in warm place until about 1 inch above top of the pan, 1 to 1½ hours.

Bake at 350° F. for 30 to 35 minutes.

SNACK WHEAT BREAD

These small slices of bread are ideal for open-faced sandwiches.

BAKE: 375° F. for 20 to 25 minutes   MAKES: 3 (12-inch) loaves

1 loaf frozen honey wheat (or pumpernickel) bread dough, thawed

Divide dough into thirds. Shape into 12-inch strips. Place 3 inches apart on greased cookie sheet. Cover; let rise in warm place until very light or doubled in size, 1 to 1½ hours.

Bake at 375° F. for 20 to 25 minutes. For open-faced sandwiches, cool and slice ¼-inch thick. Butter and top with a sandwich spread.

CARAWAY SNACK BREAD:
When shaping bread into loaevs, flatten each strip, then sprinkle each with about 1 teaspoon *caraway, anise,* or *fennel seed* and roll up into 12-inch strips.

WHEAT CHIPS:
Slice day-old Snack Wheat Bread as thin as possible (⅛ inch or less). Place on cookie sheet in single layer; dry in 250° F. oven about 1 hour, or until crisp. To serve, brush with melted *Garlic Butter,* page 120.

DOWN-TO-EARTH WHEAT BREAD

Oatmeal and raisins add a homey touch to wheat bread.

BAKE: 375° F. for 30 to 35 minutes   MAKES: 1 round loaf

1 loaf frozen honey wheat bread dough, thawed
¼ cup quick-cooking rolled oats
½ cup raisins
milk

Let dough rise slightly. Flatten to ½ inch. Sprinkle with oats and raisins. Fold in half; flatten again. Shape into round loaf. Brush loaf with milk and sprinkle with more oats. Place on greased cookie sheet. Cover; let rise in warm place until light or doubled in size, 1 to 1½ hours.

Bake at 375° F. for 30 to 35 minutes.

WHEAT GERM BREAD:
Substitute *wheat germ* for the oats; use it for sprinkling on the bread too.

DATE NUT BREAD

Honey wheat and dates complement each other in this bread.

BAKE: 350° F. for 30 to 35 minutes   MAKES: 1 loaf

1 loaf frozen honey wheat bread dough, thawed
½ cup dates, quartered
½ cup almond slices or imitation pecans
1 teaspoon grated lemon or orange peel

Let dough rise until almost doubled in size. Roll out on floured surface to a 14x7-inch rectangle. Sprinkle with dates, almonds, and peel. Fold in half; turn one quarter way around and roll out again to a 14x7-inch rectangle. Roll up, starting with 7-inch side and sealing with heels of hands after each turn. Seal ends. Place in well-greased 8x4- or 9x5-inch pan. Cover; let rise in warm place until about 1 inch above sides of pan, about 1 hour.

Bake at 350° F. for 30 to 35 minutes.

Dinner Rolls

Warm dinner rolls are good to serve with any meal, and they always add a special touch. Rolls are especially nice with luncheon meals; a large round homebaked bun makes any sandwich special!

The easy way to have homemade rolls is to start with a loaf of frozen bread dough (any flavor). For shaping most dinner rolls, it is not necessary to let the dough rise. Once it is thawed it can be divided and shaped. The only exception is when the dough needs to be rolled out. Recipe directions will say if thawing is enough or if the dough should rise. If the directions say to let the dough rise slightly, let it rise until it feels soft to the touch. Dough that has risen to double its size will rise much faster after shaping.

Use one of these methods to thaw dough:

- Place dough in the refrigerator the night before and shape about 1½ to 2 hours before it is time to bake.
- Take dough out of the freezer and let it stand at room temperature about 5 or 6 hours before shaping. For these rolls, rising time after shaping will be only 30 to 45 minutes.
- Place frozen dough in a warm place (85° to 90° F.). It will take about 3 to 3½ hours to thaw and rise, and the rising time after shaping will be 30 to 45 minutes. One loaf of bread will make 12 large to 24 medium small rolls.

After baking, rolls may be reheated in several ways. If rolls are frozen, allow an extra 15 minutes for thawing.

- Wrap rolls in foil and heat in 350° F. oven 15 minutes.
- Place rolls in brown paper bag sprinkled with a few drops of water; heat 15 minutes at 350° F.
- Place rolls on a rack in skillet; put a few tablespoons water in skillet. Cover and steam about 10 minutes.
- Heat rolls in a bun warmer.

• A microwave oven is ideal for heating dinner rolls. It will take about 15 seconds for one roll. The more rolls you have, the longer it will take. Check the manual or cookbook for your oven on the time and method. If rolls are frozen, use the defrost cycle. Place rolls on paper plate to heat.

Several companies market a frozen dinner roll. These rolls can be used to make Cloverleafs, Braids, Twin Rolls, Finger Rolls, Pan Rolls, and others. They can also be used for Breadsticks, Knots, White Mountain Rolls, Lucky Cloverleafs, Shamrock Rolls, and Posies.

Special recipes in this section which could start with frozen dinner rolls are: Hamburger Hearth Buns, Brioche Rolls, Butter Crumb Rolls, Peanut Butter Secrets, Hamburger Buns, Frankfurter Buns, and Hero Buns. You may want to experiment using them for some of the other shaping and flavor variations given in this section.

To reroll scraps of dough, first stack them and then roll them out to desired thickness.

For an extra touch, brush dinner rolls before baking with an Egg Wash, page 121, and sprinkle with sesame or poppy seed.

DINNER ROLLS

Fresh rolls will make any dinner great!

BAKE: 400° F. for 12 to 15 minutes   MAKES: 12 to 24 rolls

1 loaf frozen bread dough (any flavor except cinnamon), thawed

Shape dough as desired or directed below. Let dough rise until doubled in size, if it is to be rolled out. Place on or in a greased cookie sheet or pan. Cover; let rise in warm place until light or doubled in size, 30 to 60 minutes. (Shape-rising time may be longer if the dough is cold or has not risen before shaping.)
Bake at 400° F. for 12 to 15 minutes (or as directed) until a rich golden brown. Brush warm rolls with butter.

SHAPING DIRECTIONS:

DINNER BUNS: Divide dough into 16 to 24 pieces. Shape into balls; flatten slightly. Place 2 inches apart on greased cookie sheet. (Rolls may also be baked in well-greased muffin cups.)

PAN ROLLS: Divide dough into 16 to 24 pieces. Shape into balls. Place in rows in well-greased 9x9-, 10x8-, or 13x9 inch pan. Let rise and bake at 375° F. for 25 to 30 minutes. (Brush sides of balls of dough with *butter* for easy separation.)

FINGER ROLLS: Divide dough into 20 pieces. Shape each into 4-inch strips. *Butter* sides. Place in 2 rows in well-greased 10x8- or 9x9-inch pan. Let rise and bake at 375° F. for 25 to 30 minutes.

CLOVERLEAF ROLLS: Divide dough into 12 pieces; then divide each piece into thirds. Shape into balls; place 3 in each well-greased muffin cup.

SPEEDY CLOVERLEAFS: Divide dough into 12 pieces. Shape into balls; place in well-greased muffin cups. With greased scissors, cut rolls in halves (almost to the bottom); then cut in other direction to make quarters.

TWIN ROLLS: Divide dough into 12 pieces; then divide each piece in half. Shape into balls. Place 2 balls in greased muffin cups.

CRESCENTS: Divide dough in half. Roll out, half at a time, on floured surface to a 10-inch circle. Brush with melted *butter*. Cut into 8 or 9 wedges. Starting with wide end, roll each wedge to point. Place on greased cookie sheet, curving slightly, with point-side down.

PINWHEELS: Roll out dough on floured surface to a 15x9-inch rectangle. Brush with melted *butter*; cut into 3-inch squares. Cut diagonally from corner to within ½ inch of center. Fold alternating corners to center, overlapping slightly. Place a wooden pick in center. Place on greased cookie sheets. (Leave pick in while baking.)

KNOTS: Roll out dough on floured surface to a 16x6-inch rectangle. Cut into 6x1-inch strips; then tie strips loosely into knots. (If desired tuck ends under knot.) Place on greased cookie sheet. Brush rolls with melted *butter*.

BRAIDS: Divide dough into 15 pieces. Shape into 15-inch strips. Cut into thirds; braid together. Place on greased cookie sheet. Brush rolls with melted *butter*.

BUTTERFLAKE (FAN TAN) ROLLS: Roll out dough on floured surface to an 18x9-inch rectangle. Brush with melted *butter*. Cut into twelve 9x1½-inch strips. Stack 6 strips; cut into 1½-inch pieces for large rolls (1-inch pieces for small rolls). Place a cut-side down in greased muffin cups. Repeat with remaining strips.

WHITE MOUNTAIN ROLLS: Divide dough into 16 pieces. Shape into balls: flatten slightly. Dip tops into melted *butter,* then *flour*. Place 2 inches apart on greased cookie sheet.

CURLICUES: Roll out dough on floured surface to a 16x9-inch rectangle. Brush with melted *butter*. Roll up, starting with 16-inch side. Cut into 18 pieces. Place, cut-side down, in greased muffin cups or 2 inches apart on greased cookie sheet.

LUCKY CLOVERLEAFS: Divide dough into 12 pieces, then each piece into fourths. Shape into tiny balls; place 4 in each greased muffin cup.

PARKER HOUSE ROLLS: Roll out dough on lightly floured surface to ¼-inch thickness. Cut into rounds with 2½-inch cutter. With sharp knife, make a shallow cut slightly off center. Place a dab of melted *butter* in center. Fold small half over large half. Place on greased cookie sheet.

BUTTER TWISTS: Roll out dough on floured surface to a 15x10-inch rectangle. Brush with melted *butter*. Fold one-third of dough along 15-inch side over center. Fold other third to overlap. Cut into 1-inch strips. Twist each strip two times; place on greased cookie sheets.

DOUBLE TWISTS: Divide dough into 16 pieces. Shape into 10-inch strips. Fold in half and twist twice. Place on greased cookie sheets.

SHAMROCK ROLLS: Divide dough into 18 pieces. Roll each to a 4-inch strip. Form into ring on greased cookie sheets, sealing ends together. Make four

½-inch cuts, evenly spaced, on the outside of each ring. Brush rolls with an Egg Wash, page 119.

POSIES: Divide dough into 16 pieces. Shape into balls; flatten slightly. With greased scissors, make about six ¼-inch cuts around edge of roll. Place on greased cookie sheet. Brush with an Egg Wash, page 120; sprinkle with *sesame* or *poppy seed*.

BUTTER-CRUST ROLLS: Divide dough into 12 to 16 pieces. Shape into round or oval balls. Place 2 inches apart on greased cookie sheet. With sharp knife, make a ¼-inch cut across tops. Place about ½ teaspoon *butter* in each cut.

HAMBURGER BUNS

Freshly baked buns for hamburgers or frankfurters make an easy supper good enough for a company meal.

BAKE: 400° F. for 12 to 15 minutes   MAKES: 12 buns

1 loaf frozen white bread dough, thawed (honey wheat, pumpernickel, and French frozen doughs make deluxe buns)

Divide dough into 12 pieces. Shape into balls; flatten slightly. Place 3 inches apart on greased cookie sheet. Cover; let rise in warm place until very light or doubled in size, 1 to 1½ hours.

Bake at 400° F. for 12 to 15 minutes.

SUPER-HAMBURGER BUNS:
Make 8 to 10 buns from a loaf. Flatten. Brush with a mixture of egg and a small amount of water; then sprinkle with *sesame seed*. Cut an X on the top.

FRANKFURTER BUNS:
Shape pieces of dough into buns about 4 inches long and 1 inch wide; flatten. Let rise and bake.

BUTTER CRUMB ROLLS

Crunchy coated buns that are great for sandwiches. Or make them bigger for hamburger buns.

BAKE: 375° F. for 15 to 20 minutes   MAKES: 12 rolls

1 loaf frozen (any flavor) bread dough, thawed
⅓ cup bread crumbs (or ready-to-eat cereal, crushed)
1 teaspoon poppy seed, caraway, or mixed herbs
2 tablespoons butter or margarine, melted

Divide dough into 12 pieces. Shape into balls. Combine crumbs and seeds. Coat balls with butter, then crumbs. Place 3 inches apart on greased cookie sheet. Flatten slightly. Cover; let rise in warm place until light or doubled in size, 1 to 1½ hours.

Bake at 375° F. for 15 to 20 minutes.

SHORT-CUT IDEA: If you do not want to shape rolls, dip pieces of dough into butter; then coat with crumbs.

TWO-TONE TWIN ROLLS

For a novel roll, combine pieces of white and honey wheat dough to make a variety of shapes.

BAKE: 400° F. for 12 to 15 minutes   MAKES: 24 to 30 rolls

1 loaf frozen white bread dough, thawed
1 loaf frozen honey wheat bread dough, thawed

Divide each loaf into 12 to 15 pieces; then cut each piece in half. Shape into balls. Place a white and honey wheat ball in each greased muffin cup (or place the 2 balls close together on greased cookie sheet). Cover; let rise in warm place until doubled in size, 1½ to 2 hours.

Bake at 400° F. for 12 to 15 minutes.

TIP: If desired, brush rolls with an Egg Wash, page 121, and sprinkle with sesame seed.

CLOVERLEAF ROLLS:
Divide each of the 12 or 15 pieces of dough into 3 pieces. Shape into tiny balls. Place 3 balls (2 or 1 white and 1 or 2 honey wheat) in each greased muffin cup.

BRAIDED ROLLS:
Divide dough as for Cloverleaf Rolls. Shape each piece into 4-inch strips. Braid 3 strips together, using both white and honey wheat in each braid.

MARBLE ROLLS:
Divide dough as for Twin Rolls. Take a small piece of white and honey wheat and shape the two into one ball. Place 2 inches apart on greased cookie sheets.

PINWHEEL ROLLS:
Let dough rise until almost doubled in size. Divide each loaf in half. Place one white half on top of a honey wheat half. Flatten slightly on floured surface; roll out to a 16x10-inch rectangle. Brush with melted *butter*. Roll up, starting with 16-inch side. Cut into 15 pieces. Place, cut-side down, in greased muffin cups or on greased cookie sheet. Repeat with remaining dough.

Dinner Rolls:
  1. *Super-Hamburger Buns*
  2. *Two-Tone Twin Rolls*
  3. *Posies*
  4. *Knots*
  5. *White Mountain Rolls*
  6. *Double Twists*
  7. *Herb Butter*
  8. *Double Cheese Pinwheels*
  9. *Bacon Cheese Crescents*
 10. *Hero Buns*
 11. *Dinner Buns*
 12. *English Muffins*
 13. *Finger Rolls*
 14. *Breadsticks*

HERB ROLLS

A garni of herbs blended into these rolls makes them especially good with roast beef or pork.

BAKE: 400° F. for 12 to 15 minutes   MAKES: 16 rolls

1 loaf frozen white bread dough, thawed
herbs—parsley, oregano, thyme, marjoram, basil, chives

Let dough rise until doubled in size. Roll out on floured surface to ¼-inch thickness. Sprinkle generously with 3 or more of the suggested herbs; fold in half. Roll out again and cut into 16 squares. Shape into balls. Place 2 inches apart on greased cookie sheet or close together in well-greased 9-inch square pan. Cover; let rise in warm place until light or doubled in size, 30 to 60 minutes.

Bake at 400° F. for 12 to 15 minutes. (Bake at 375° for 20 to 25 minutes if 9-inch pan is used.) Brush hot rolls with plain or garlic butter.

DINNER ROLL FLAVOR VARIATIONS:
For other flavors in dinner rolls, omit the herbs and sprinkle with one of the combinations suggested below. Shape, let rise, and bake as for Herb Rolls.

ONION-DILL: 2 tablespoons finely chopped *onion*, 1 teaspoon *dill weed*

CHEESE-CARAWAY: ½ cup shredded *cheese*, 1 teaspoon *caraway seed*

BACON: ½ cup crumbled fried *bacon*

GARLIC: sprinkle of *garlic powder*

ORANGE-ANISE: 1 tablespoon grated *orange peel*, 1 teaspoon *anise seed*

SMOKY-BARBECUE: brush dough lightly with *smoke sauce;* sprinkle with *barbecue seasoned salt*

DOUBLE CHEESE PINWHEELS

Two kinds of cheese are combined to flavor these rolls.

BAKE: 375° F. for 15 to 18 minutes   MAKES: 16 rolls

1 loaf frozen white (or honey wheat) bread dough, thawed
2 tablespoons butter or margarine, melted
¼ cup Parmesan cheese
¼ cup shredded Cheddar cheese
½ teaspoon dill weed, if desired

Let dough rise until doubled in size. Roll out on floured surface to a 16-inch square. Brush with butter. Combine cheeses and dill; sprinkle over dough. Cut into sixteen 4-inch squares. Make diagonal cuts from each corner to ½ inch of center. Fold alternating corners to center, overlapping slightly. Place on greased cookie sheets. Insert wooden pick in center of each to hold points down. Cover; let rise in warm place until light, 30 to 60 minutes.

Bake at 375° F. for 15 to 18 minutes. Best warm.

HERO BUNS

Large buns that make good submarine, torpedo, or poor boy
sandwiches. A good summer supper after the baseball game.
Fill rolls early and refrigerate.

BAKE: 375° F. for 20 to 25 minutes   MAKES: 6 or 8 rolls

1 loaf frozen white (French or honey wheat) bread dough, thawed
1 tablespoon egg
1 tablespoon water
sesame or poppy seed

Divide dough into 6 or 8 pieces. Shape into oblong or round buns. Place
3 inches apart on greased cookie sheet. Make a cut or two across top
of each. Combine egg and water; brush on rolls. Sprinkle with seeds.
Cover; let rise in warm place until light or doubled in size, 1 to 1½ hours.

Bake at 375° F. for 20 to 25 minutes.

TO SERVE: Split, butter, and fill with lettuce, cold cuts of meat, cheese,
pickles, and tomatoes. If you want to serve warm, omit lettuce; wrap in
foil and heat in 350° F. oven about 15 minutes.

OTHER GOOD FILLINGS: Egg or tuna salad; tuna and cheese, heated
or broiled; beans and wieners; barbecued beef; sloppy Joe filling.

GARDEN ROLLS

Bits of chopped or grated fresh vegetables add a calico touch
and a fun flavor to rolls. Make them large for a sandwich or
hamburger bun; make them small for a snack roll.

BAKE: 375° F. for 15 to 18 minutes   MAKES: 12 to 20 rolls

1 loaf frozen white (or honey wheat) bread dough, thawed
1 carrot, pared and shredded
2 tablespoons chopped fresh parsley or chives
2 tablespoons finely chopped green pepper
1 tablesoon finely minced onion
butter
seasoned salt

Let dough rise until almost doubled in size. Flatten to about ¼-inch
thickness. Sprinkle with vegetables and seasoned salt; press down firmly.
Cut into 12 to 20 pieces. Shape into balls, keeping vegetables covered.
Place 2 inches apart on greased cookie sheet. Cover; let rise in warm
place until light or doubled in size, about 1 hour.

Bake at 375° F. for 15 to 18 minutes. Brush warm rolls with butter;
sprinkle with seasoned salt. Freeze or refrigerate leftover rolls.

DOUBLE-QUICK DINNER ROLLS

If shaping rolls frightens you, then you're going to like these rolls; they need no shaping whatsoever.

BAKE: 400° F. for 12 to 15 minutes   MAKES: 12 to 18 rolls

1 loaf frozen bread dough (any flavor except cinnamon), thawed
1 tablespoon egg
1 tablespoon water
sesame seed or poppy seed

Divide dough into 12 to 18 pieces, depending on size and number of rolls desired. Place in well-greased muffin cups or about 2 inches apart on greased cookie sheet. Combine egg and water; brush tops of rolls. Sprinkle with sesame seed. Cover; let rise in warm place until light or doubled in size, 1½ to 2 hours.

Bake at 400° F. for 12 to 15 minutes.

BREADSTICKS

Breadsticks are good with soup, salad, and Italian entrées. Or serve them as a snack with a chip dip.

BAKE: 425° F. for 12 to 15 minutes   MAKES: 24 sticks

1 loaf frozen white (or French) bread dough, thawed
1 tablespoon egg or egg white
1 tablespoon water
coarse salt, caraway, sesame, or poppy seed

Let dough rise until doubled in size. Divide into 24 pieces. Shape into pencil-like strips 12 inches long. Place 1 inch apart on greased cookie sheets. Let rise in warm place 30 minutes. If sticks shorten while rising, stretch to the 12-inch length. Combine egg and water; carefully brush over sticks. Sprinkle with salt.

Bake at 425° F. for 12 to 15 minutes or until a rich golden brown. For crisper sticks, turn off oven heat and leave in oven 10 minutes.

Trick: Use cookie sheet with no sides. Place sticks crosswise; hook a small amount of ends over edge of sheet.

ONION RINGS

Onion soup and sour cream are twisted into these dinner rolls.
Good with chicken.

BAKE: 400° F. for 12 to 15 minutes   MAKES: 18 rolls

1 loaf frozen white (or honey wheat) bread dough, thawed
1 package dry onion soup mix
1 cup dairy sour cream

Let dough rise until doubled in size. Combine soup mix and sour
cream. Roll out dough on floured surface to an 18x10-inch rectangle.
Brush half of dough along 18-inch side with filling. Fold uncovered half
over filling. Cut into 1-inch strips. Twist 4 or 5 times; form into circle
and seal ends together. Place on greased cookie sheets. Cover; let rise
in warm place until light, 30 to 60 minutes.

Bake at 400° F. 12 to 15 minutes. Best warm. Refrigerate or freeze
leftover rolls.

BRIOCHE ROLLS

These rolls take on the shape of French brioche.

BAKE: 400° F. for 12 to 15 minutes   MAKES: 12 rolls

1 loaf frozen white bread dough, thawed
1 tablespoon egg
1 teaspoon water

Cut off a scant fourth of dough. Divide remaining dough into 12 pieces.
Shape into balls; place in well-greased 3-inch tart pans or muffin cups.
Divide remaining dough into 12 pieces and shape into tiny balls. With
scissors, snip a deep hole in center of large balls. Taper one side of small
ball and insert into large ball. Combine egg and water; brush over rolls.
Cover; let rise in warm place until very light or doubled in size, 1 to 1½
hours. (If top ball rolls to side, carefully place on top of roll.)

Bake at 400° F. for 12 to 15 minutes.

HAMBURGER HEARTH BUNS

*A touch of the Old World glamorizes buns for hamburgers—
makes them gourmet fare.*

BAKE: 400° F. for 12 to 15 minutes   MAKES: 10 large buns

1 loaf frozen white (or French) bread dough, thawed
melted butter or margarine
flour
seasoned salt

Divide dough into 10 pieces. Shape into balls; flatten slightly. Dip tops
into butter and then into flour to coat generously. Place 3 inches apart
on greased cookie sheet. Sprinkle with salt. Cover; let rise in warm place
until light or doubled in size, 1 to 1½ hours.

Bake at 400° F. for 12 to 15 minutes. Use as hamburger buns or as buns
for sandwich meats and cheeses.

BACON CHEESE CRESCENTS

*Rolls crunchy with bacon and cheese are good for lunch or for
any lighter meal.*

BAKE: 375° F. for 15 to 18 minutes   MAKES: 18 rolls

1 loaf frozen white bread dough, thawed
1 tablespoon butter, melted
½ cup shredded Cheddar cheese
4 slices bacon, fried and crumbled

Let dough rise until doubled in size. Roll out, half at a time, on lightly
floured surface to a 10-inch circle. Brush with butter; sprinkle with cheese
and bacon. Cut each round into 9 wedges. Starting with wide end, roll
each wedge to point. Place, point-side down, on greased cookie sheet.
Cover; let rise in warm place until very light or doubled in size, 30 to 45
minutes.

Bake at 375° F. for 15 to 18 minutes. Refrigerate or freeze leftover rolls.

ENGLISH MUFFINS

Small round buns or muffins baked on a griddle, then split and toasted before serving. They were once served by vendors on the streets of England.

BAKE: medium hot griddle 10 to 15 minutes   MAKES: 12 to 15 muffins

1 loaf frozen white bread dough, thawed
(frozen French or honey wheat doughs make good muffins)

Let dough rise until doubled in size. Roll out on surface sprinkled with flour and corn meal to ¼-inch thickness. Cut into rounds with 3-inch cutter. Place 1 inch apart on cookie sheet sprinkled with cornmeal. Cover; let rise in warm place until light or doubled in size, 30 to 45 minutes.

Bake on medium hot griddle or skillet (350° F.) 10 to 15 minutes, turning once to brown both sides. To serve, split and toast, and then butter and spread with jelly, jam, honey, peanut butter, or cinnamon sugar.

ENGLISH MUFFIN SUPPER IDEAS:

English Muffins are delicious toasted and topped with a rarebit sauce, au gratin tuna or à la king sauce. Or use them to make open-faced grilled cheese sandwiches, Reubens, and other sandwiches.

CHEESE RAREBIT: Melt 2 tablespoons *butter* in saucepan; stir in 2 tablespoons *flour*. Add 1 cup *milk;* cook, stirring constantly, until thickened. Blend in 1 cup shredded Cheddar *cheese,* ½ teaspoon *salt,* and a pinch of *pepper.* If desired, add 1 cup cubed cooked *meat* or *fish* (ham, chicken, turkey, or tuna). Reheat. Serve over hot toasted muffin halves. Makes 4 to 6 servings.

À LA KING SAUCE: Melt 3 tablespoons *butter* or margarine in saucepan; stir in 3 tablespoons *flour.* Gradually add 1½ cups *milk* (part half and half); cook, stirring constantly, until thickened. Add 2 teaspoons *chicken bouillon granules,* ⅛ teaspoon white *pepper,* ½ cup cooked or canned *mushrooms,* and 1 cup cooked *meat* or *fish* (turkey, ham, chicken, tuna, shrimp). Reheat. Serve over hot toasted muffin halves. Makes 6 to 8 servings.

TUNA CHEESE TOPPERS: Combine 1 (6½ oz.) can drained *tuna,* 2 tablespoons *salad dressing,* ½ teaspoon *dill seed* or *dill weed,* and 1 tablespoon finely chopped *chives.* Place a spoonful on top of toasted muffin halves. Top with a *tomato* slice and a *cheese* slice. Place under broiler until cheese melts. Makes 8 sandwiches.

BOLOGNA CHEESE QUICKIES: Combine 1 cup chopped *bologna* and 1 cup shredded *cheese.* Place on toasted muffin halves. Broil until cheese melts. Makes 12 sandwiches.

EASY PIZZA MUFFINS: Spread your favorite *pizza sauce* or topping on muffin halves; then top with *salami strip* and shredded pizza *cheese.* Broil until cheese melts.

PEANUT BUTTER SECRETS

Rolls stuffed with peanut butter make a great after-school treat.

BAKE: 400° F. for 12 to 15 minutes   MAKES: 20 rolls

1 loaf frozen white (raisin or honey wheat) bread dough, thawed
peanut butter

Let dough rise slightly. Divide into 20 pieces. Flatten each piece and top with a teaspoonful peanut butter. Bring dough around filling. Seal and shape into ball. Place 2 inches apart on greased cookie sheet. Cover; let rise in warm place until light or doubled in size, 1 to 1½ hours.

Bake at 400° F. for 12 to 15 minutes.

PEANUT AU CHOCOLAT SECRETS:
Seal 3 or 4 *semi-sweet chocolate pieces* inside rolls with the peanut butter.

PEANUT BUTTER ROLLS

Peanut butter adds extra nutrition to a dinner, supper, or mid-afternoon snack roll.

BAKE: 375° F. for 15 to 18 minutes   MAKES: 16 rolls

1 loaf frozen white (or honey wheat) bread dough, thawed
½ cup peanut butter

Let dough rise until doubled in size. Roll out on floured surface to 16x10-inch rectangle. Spread half, along 16-inch side, with peanut butter. Fold uncovered half over peanut butter. Cut into 1-inch strips. Twist each 4 or 5 times; coil onto greased cookie sheet, tucking end under. Cover; let rise in warm place until light, 30 to 60 minutes.

Bake at 375° F. for 15 to 18 minutes.

HONEY ROLLS

Honey butter adds the final touch to these rolls.

BAKE: 375° F. for 15 to 20 minutes   MAKES: 18 rolls

1 loaf frozen white (or honey wheat) bread dough, thawed
3 tablespoons butter or margarine, soft or melted
nutmeg
¼ cup honey

Let dough rise until doubled in size. Roll out on floured surface to an 18x10-inch rectangle. Brush with half the butter; sprinkle lightly with nutmeg. Roll up, starting with 18-inch side. Cut into 18 pieces. Place, cut-side down, in well-greased muffin cups or 13x9-inch pan. Cover; let rise in warm place until very light or doubled in size, 30 to 45 minutes. Combine remaining butter and honey. Brush carefully over risen rolls.

Bake at 375° F. for 15 to 20 minutes. Remove from pan immediately.

Sweet Rolls

The variety of sweet rolls that can be made from a one-pound loaf of frozen bread dough is unlimited. You can substitute a loaf of frozen dough for most sweet roll recipes that use about three cups of flour.

If you're looking for something easy to start with in sweet rolls, try Cinnamon Buns, page 44. There's no shaping—all you do is cut off a piece of dough, coat it with butter and then cinnamon sugar, and place it in a muffin cup to rise. You end up with cinnamon sugar all the way around. Cinnamon and caramel rolls have always been favorite sweet rolls, but let's not stop there. Surprise your family with something completely new in sweet rolls.

When making sweet rolls, it is convenient to take the dough out of the freezer the night before and let it thaw in the refrigerator. Let it stand at room temperature at least one hour to warm and rise to about double in size. Any dough that is to be rolled out on a floured surface is easier to handle if it has doubled in size. Some brands of frozen bread dough are easier to roll out than others.

To bake sweet rolls on cookie sheets, line them with foil and then grease. This makes clean-up easier.

The easy way to divide dough into equal pieces is to first cut the dough in half and then cut the halves in half. Next cut each of these pieces into one-fourth of the total number called for in the recipe. Or, if the total number of pieces needed for the recipe is divisible by 3, start by dividing the whole piece into thirds.

For more suggestions on working with frozen doughs see the Know-How section at the beginning of this book.

When there are scraps of dough to reroll, stack them and then roll them out to the desired thickness. Or you may just want to shape these small pieces of dough into a dinner roll or two.

To dust rolls or coffee cake with powdered sugar, place sugar in a small sieve and press through with finger or spoon. This eliminates lumps and lets you dust evenly.

In the frozen bread dough section at your supermarket, you may find a sweet yeast bread dough. This is specifically developed for use in making your favorite sweet rolls and coffee cakes. When you want a richer and sweeter dough, use it to make any of the recipes in this book.

However, this frozen yeast sweet bread dough may not be available in all areas of the country. Another frozen yeast dough that you may want to try with some of the sweet roll recipes, especially cinnamon rolls, is frozen raisin bread dough.

CINNAMON BUNS

You'll like to make these easy cinnamon rolls—no rolling.

BAKE: 375° F. for 15 to 20 minutes   MAKES: 18 rolls

1 loaf frozen white (or sweet) bread dough, thawed
¼ cup butter or margarine, melted
½ cup sugar
¼ cup finely chopped nuts
1 teaspoon cinnamon

Divide dough into 18 pieces. Roll in butter and then in a mixture of the sugar, nuts, and cinnamon. Place in well-greased muffin cups. Cover; let rise in warm place until light or doubled in size, about 1½ hours.

Bake at 375° F. for 15 to 20 minutes. Remove from pans immediately. If desired, frost with Vanilla Icing, page 118.

BUTTERSCOTCH NUT BUNS:
Place ¼ teaspoon *water* in each well-greased muffin cup, then 1 teaspoon chopped *nuts*. Melt ¼ cup *butter*. Combine ¼ cup *granulated sugar*, ¼ cup *brown sugar*, and ½ teaspoon *cinnamon*. Coat pieces of dough first with butter and then with sugar mixture. Place on top of the nuts. Let rise and bake.

ORANGE BUNS:
Place 1 teaspoon *orange juice* in each well-greased muffin cup. Melt ¼ cup *butter*. Combine ½ cup *sugar*, 1 tablespoon grated *orange peel*, and ¼ cup *coconut*, if desired. Coat pieces of dough first with butter and then with orange-sugar mixture. Let rise and bake.

SUGGESTION: If desired, any of the above rolls may be baked in a well-greased 9x9-, 10x8-, or 13x9-inch pan. For the Butterscotch Buns, sprinkle 1 tablespoon water in pan; for the Orange Buns, ¼ cup orange juice.

MOM'S CINNAMON ROLLS

*Slightly caramelly cinnamon rolls developed from the rolls my
mother used to make for a Sunday special.*

BAKE: 375° F. for 20 to 25 minutes   MAKES: 12 to 16 rolls

1 loaf frozen white (or sweet) bread dough, thawed
3 tablespoons butter or margarine, melted
3 tablespoons granulated sugar
3 tablespoons brown sugar
1 teaspoon cinnamon
½ cup chopped nuts, if desired

Let dough rise until doubled in size. Sprinkle nuts into buttered 9x9- or
10x8-inch pan. Roll out dough on floured surface to a 15x10-inch rectangle. Brush with butter; sprinkle with remaining ingredients. Roll up,
starting with 15-inch side. Cut into 12 to 16 pieces. Place, cut-side down,
in pan. Cover; let rise in warm place until light or doubled in size, 30 to
60 minutes.

Bake at 375° F. for 20 to 25 minutes, or until light golden brown. Immediately turn out onto rack.

TINY CINNAMON ROLLS

Just the right size for a reception or a brunch.

BAKE: 375° F. for 15 to 20 minutes   MAKES: 40 rolls

1 loaf frozen white (or sweet) bread dough, thawed
¼ cup butter or margarine, melted
½ cup sugar
2 teaspoons cinnamon
½ cup finely chopped nuts, if desired

Let dough rise until doubled in size. Roll out on floured surface to an
18x10-inch rectangle. Combine sugar and cinnamon. Brush dough with
half the butter; sprinkle with half the cinnamon-sugar mixture and all
the nuts. Cut in half lengthwise to make two 18x5-inch rectangles. Roll
up each. Cut each strip into 20 pieces. Place, cut-side down, in well-
greased 13x9- or 15x10-inch pan. Brush with remaining butter; then
sprinkle with remaining cinnamon sugar. Cover; let rise in warm place
until doubled in size, 30 to 60 minutes.

Bake at 375° F. for 15 to 20 minutes. Remove from pan immediately.
Frost warm rolls with one of the icings on page 118.

MINI-ORANGE ROLLS:
Substitute 2 tablespoons grated *orange peel* for the cinnamon. Omit the
nuts and use coconut. Frost with Orange Icing, page 118.

SWEDISH CINNAMON ROLLS

The all time favorite sweet roll takes on a new shape when you bake the Swedish way.

BAKE: 375° F. for 20 to 25 minutes   MAKES: 20 rolls

1 loaf frozen white (or sweet) bread dough, thawed
5 tablespoons butter or margarine, melted
½ cup sugar
2 teaspoons cinnamon
¼ cup finely chopped nuts, if desired

Let dough rise until doubled in size. Butter a 13x9-inch pan. Combine sugar, cinnamon, and nuts. Roll out dough on floured surface to a 20x10-inch rectangle. Brush with half the butter. Sprinkle with two-thirds of cinnamon-sugar mixture. Roll up, starting with 20-inch side. Cut into 20 pieces. Place, cut-side down, in buttered pan. Brush tops with remaining butter; sprinkle with rest of cinnamon sugar. Cover; let rise in warm place until light and doubled in size, 30 to 60 minutes.

Bake at 375° F. for 20 to 25 minutes.

CINNAMON PALM LEAVES:
Cut rolled up dough into 1½-inch pieces. Make 2 cuts, ½-inch apart, almost to opposite side. Spread slices to make a fan shape; place on greased cookie sheet. Brush tops with remaining butter; sprinkle with rest of cinnamon sugar. Let rise and bake 15 to 18 minutes.

BUTTERFLY CINNAMON ROLLS:
Cut rolled up dough into 1½-inch pieces. Place, seam-side down, 3 inches apart on greased cookie sheet. With fork handle, press down center of each roll all the way to bottom. Brush with remaining butter; sprinkle with remaining cinnamon sugar. Let rise and bake 15 to 18 minutes.

Sweet Rolls:
1. Sweet Cloverleafs
2. Sunday Best Rolls
3. Doughnut Knots
4. Danish "S" Rolls
5. Danish Coffee Rolls
6. Open-faced Kolackies
7. Cherry Streusel Triangles
8. Cookie Buns
9. Raised Doughnuts
10. Mom's Cinnamon Rolls
11. Cinnamon Daisies
12. Elephant Ears

CINNAMON JELLY ROLLS

Cinnamon rolls glistening with their jelly centers will satisfy many hungry appetites.

BAKE: 375° F. for 15 to 18 minutes   MAKES: 16 rolls

1 loaf frozen white (or sweet) bread dough, thawed
2 tablespoons butter or margarine, melted
⅓ cup sugar
1 tablespoon brown sugar
1 teaspoon cinnamon
jelly or jam

Let dough rise until doubled in size. Roll out on floured surface to a 16x10-inch rectangle. Brush with most of the butter. Combine sugars and cinnamon. Sprinkle all but 1 tablespoon over dough. Roll up, starting with 16-inch side. Cut into 16 pieces. Place, cut-side down, on cookie sheet lined with foil and greased. Flatten roll with hands to about ¼ inch. Brush with butter and sprinkle with the rest of the cinnamon sugar. Place a half-teaspoon jelly or jam in the center of each roll. Cover; let rise in warm place until doubled in size, 30 to 60 minutes.

Bake at 375° F. for 15 to 18 minutes. If desired, frost with one of the icings on page 118.

CINNAMON DAISIES

Jelly forms the center of these cinnamon-coated posies.

BAKE: 375° F. for 12 to 15 minutes   MAKES: 15 to 18 rolls

1 loaf frozen white (or sweet) bread dough, thawed
1 tablespoon butter or margarine, melted
¼ cup sugar
1 teaspoon cinnamon
jelly or jam

Let dough rise until doubled in size. Roll out on floured surface to ¼-inch thickness. Cut into rounds with a 2½-inch cutter. Brush tops with butter. Combine cinnamon and sugar. Dip tops into cinnamon-sugar mixture. Place on well-greased cookie sheets. With scissors, make 6 cuts (½ inch deep) around edge of each roll. Cover; let rise in warm place until light or doubled in size, 30 to 45 minutes.

Punch deep hole in center of each roll with floured fingers; fill with ½ teaspoon jelly. Bake at 375° F. for 12 to 15 minutes. Frost warm rolls with Vanilla Icing, page 118.

ELEPHANT EARS

An easy way to make this favorite thin sugary-crisp roll.

BAKE: 375° F. for 15 to 18 minutes   MAKES: 16 rolls

1 loaf frozen white (or sweet) bread dough, thawed
3 tablespoons butter or margarine, melted
¾ cup sugar
2 tablespoons brown sugar
2 teaspoons cinnamon

Let dough rise until doubled in size. Combine sugars and cinnamon. Roll out dough on floured surface to a 16x12-inch rectangle. Brush with half the butter and sprinkle with 2 tablespoons of the sugar mixture. Fold in half; roll out again to 16x12-inch rectangle. Brush with remaining butter and sprinkle with 2 tablespoons of the sugar mixture. Roll up, starting with 16-inch side. Cut into 16 pieces. Sprinkle rolling surface with sugar mixture. Roll out each piece to ⅛ to ¼ inch, turning to coat both sides with sugar. Place on well-greased cookie sheets. Let rise 15 minutes.

Bake at 375° F. for 15 to 18 minutes.

DANISH BUTTER CRISPIES:
Omit brown sugar and decrease cinnamon to ½ teaspoon. Add ½ cup *almond slices* to the sugar mixture.

ORANGE SUGAR CRISPIES:
Substitute 2 teaspoons grated *orange peel* for cinnamon and, if desired, add ½ cup flaked or grated *coconut* to the sugar mixture.

SWEET CLOVERLEAFS

Three twirls instead of one make up these caramel-like cinnamon rolls. They look triply special.

BAKE: 375° F. for 15 to 18 minutes   MAKES: 12 rolls

1 loaf frozen white (or sweet) bread dough, thawed
3 tablespoons butter or margarine, melted
½ cup sugar (half brown)
1 ½ teaspoons cinnamon

Let dough rise until doubled in size. Butter 12 muffin cups. Roll out dough on floured surface to a 14-inch square. Brush with remaining butter. Combine sugars and cinnamon; sprinkle over dough. Cut into three strips. Roll up each, starting with 14-inch side. Cut each into 12 pieces. Place 3 pieces, cut-side down, in each greased muffin cup. Cover; let rise in warm place until very light, 30 to 60 minutes.

Bake at 375° F. for 15 to 18 minutes. Remove from pans immediately.

ORANGE STICKY ROLLS

A good brunch roll to serve with a main dish salad.

BAKE: 375° F. for 20 to 25 minutes   MAKES: 15 or 16 rolls

1 loaf frozen white (sweet or honey wheat) bread dough, thawed
2 tablespoons butter or margarine, melted
¼ cup sugar
¼ cup light corn syrup
¼ cup orange juice
1 tablespoon soft butter or margarine
1 tablespoon grated orange peel
nutmeg or mace

Let dough rise until doubled in size. Combine melted butter, sugar, syrup, and juice. Spread in well-buttered 10x8- or 9x9-inch pan. Roll out dough on floured surface to a 15x12-inch rectangle. Brush with soft butter; sprinkle with peel and nutmeg. Roll up, starting with 15-inch side. Cut into 15 or 16 pieces. Place, cut-side down, in prepared pan. Cover; let rise in warm place until light or doubled in size, 30 to 60 minutes.

Bake at 375° F. for 20 to 25 minutes. Loosen edges immediately and turn onto wire rack over waxed paper.

SUGGESTION: For flatter and more crusty rolls, use a 13x9-inch pan. Cut the 15-inch roll into 18 or 20 pieces and place in the prepared pan.

SUNDAY BEST ROLLS

Sweet rolls that look so special and taste so good it's hard to believe they can be so simple to make.

BAKE: 375° F. for 20 to 25 minutes   MAKES: 15 rolls

1 loaf frozen white (or sweet) bread dough, thawed
½ cup sugar (half brown)
¼ teaspoon nutmeg
¼ teaspoon cinnamon
¼ cup soft or melted butter or margarine
jam or preserves

Let dough rise until doubled in size. Brush 13x9-inch pan with half the butter. Combine sugars and spices. Roll out dough on floured surface to 15-inch square; sprinkle with half the sugar mixture. Fold in half. Roll out to 15x12-inch rectangle. Brush with remaining butter and sprinkle with remaining sugar mixture. Roll up, starting with 15-inch side. Cut into 15 rolls. Flatten each roll with rolling pin to ¼ inch. Place in pan. Cover; let rise in warm place until light or doubled in size, 30 to 60 minutes. Place a spoonful of jam in center of each roll.

Bake at 375° F. for 20 to 25 minutes. Remove from pan immediately. Frost with Vanilla Icing, page 118.

CARAMEL NUT ROLLS

The old-fashioned gooey pecan roll is always a favorite. Light molasses or honey adds just a slight variation in the flavor.

BAKE: 375° F. for 25 to 30 minutes   MAKES: 15 or 16 rolls

1 loaf frozen white (or sweet) bread dough, thawed
4 tablespoons butter or margarine, melted
½ cup brown sugar
2 teaspoons water
2 tablespoons light corn syrup
½ cup broken pecans or walnuts
cinnamon

Let dough rise until doubled in size. Brush a 10x8- or 9x9-inch pan with 1 tablespoon butter. Combine 2 tablespoons butter, ¼ cup brown sugar, water, and corn syrup. Spread in pan. Sprinkle with pecans. Roll out dough on floured surface to a 16x12-inch rectangle. Brush with remaining butter and sprinkle with ¼ cup brown sugar and cinnamon. Roll up, starting with 16-inch side. Cut into 15 or 16 pieces. Place, cut-side down, in pan. Cover; let rise in warm place until light, 30 to 60 minutes.

Bake at 375° F. for 25 to 30 minutes. Cool 1 minute. Loosen edges and turn out onto wire rack lined with waxed paper.

TAFFY ROLLS:
Substitute *light molasses* or dark corn syrup for the light corn syrup. Use *coconut* instead of nuts.

HONEY BUNS:
Substitute *honey* for the corn syrup.

GRANDMA'S RAISIN SUGAR ROLLS

A touch of sweetness and lots of raisins make this old-fashioned roll a youngster's favorite.

BAKE: 375° F. for 20 to 25 minutes   MAKES: 15 or 16 rolls

1 loaf frozen white (or sweet) bread dough, thawed
2 tablespoons butter or margarine, melted
¼ cup sugar
cinnamon or nutmeg
½ cup raisins

Let dough rise until doubled in size. Roll out on floured surface to a 15x10-inch rectangle. Brush with butter; sprinkle with remaining ingredients. Roll up, starting with 15-inch side. Cut into 15 or 16 rolls. Place, cut-side down, in well-buttered 9x9- or 10x8-inch pan. Cover; let rise in warm place until light or doubled in size, 30 to 60 minutes.

Bake at 375° F. for 20 to 25 minutes, or until light golden brown. Remove from pan immediately. Frost warm rolls with one of the icings on page 118.

MAPLE NUT WHEAT ROLLS

The maple-flavored caramel syrup is a perfect combination with the honey wheat bread.

BAKE: 350° F. for 25 to 30 minutes   MAKES: 15 or 16 rolls

1 loaf frozen honey wheat bread dough, thawed
4 tablespoons butter or margarine, melted
⅓ cup and 2 tablespoons brown sugar
3 tablespoons maple-flavored syrup
¼ teaspoon maple flavor extract, if desired
½ cup broken walnuts or pecans
cinnamon

Let dough rise until doubled in size. Combine 2 tablespoons butter, ⅓ cup brown sugar, syrup, and extract; spread in well-buttered 10x8- or 9x9-inch pan. Sprinkle with nuts. Roll out dough on floured surface to 15x10-inch rectangle. Brush with remaining butter; then sprinkle with 2 tablespoons brown sugar and cinnamon. Roll up, starting with 15-inch side. Cut into 15 or 16 pieces. Place, cut-side down, in prepared pan. Cover; let rise in warm place until light or doubled in size, 30 to 60 minutes.

Bake at 350° F. for 25 to 30 minutes. Let stand 30 seconds. Loosen edges and turn out onto rack lined with waxed paper.

HONEY WHEAT ROLLS:
Substitute honey for the maple syrup.

JELLY ROLLS

The swirl of jelly makes these a good lunch or breakfast roll.

BAKE: 375° F. for 15 to 18 minutes   MAKES: 18 rolls

1 loaf frozen white (sweet or honey wheat) bread dough, thawed
1 tablespoon soft or melted butter
½ cup preserves, jelly, or marmalade
2 tablespoons bread or graham cracker crumbs

Let dough rise until doubled in size. Roll out on floured surface to an 18x10-inch rectangle. Brush with butter, then preserves. Sprinkle with crumbs. Roll up, starting with 18-inch side. Cut into 18 pieces. Place, cut-side down, in well-greased muffin cups. Cover; let rise in warm place until light or doubled in size, 30 to 60 minutes.

Bake at 375° F. for 15 to 18 minutes. Loosen and turn out immediately.

NOTE: Rolls may be baked in greased 13x9-inch pan. Bake 20 to 25 minutes.

PEANUT BUTTER JELLY ROLLS:
Combine ¼ cup *peanut butter* and ¼ cup *jelly;* substitute for preserves in above recipe.

FIGURE EIGHTS

Sugar-coated strips of dough are coiled to take on an eight shape.

BAKE: 375° F. for 15 to 18 minutes   MAKES: 16 rolls

1 loaf frozen white (or sweet) bread dough, thawed
¼ cup butter or margarine, melted
⅓ cup sugar
1 teaspoon cinnamon

Let dough rise until doubled in size. Divide into 16 pieces. Combine sugar and cinnamon. Shape each dough piece into 10-inch strips. Dip into butter; then coat with cinnamon-sugar mixture. Place in shape of an "8" on greased cookie sheet. Cover; let rise in warm place until light, 30 to 60 minutes.

Bake at 375° F. for 15 to 18 minutes. Remove from sheet immediately.

CINNAMON SNAILS:
Coil the strips onto greased cookie sheet, 2 inches apart. If desired, place a spoonful of jelly in the center of each hot baked roll. Frost with one of the icings on page 118.

SWEET KNOTS:
Tie the sugar-coated strips into knots. Place on greased sheet, tucking ends under.

SWEET WHIRLUPS:
Drop each sugar-coated strip into a greased muffin cup and allow to spread casually.

GLAZED LEMON ROLLS

The lemon touch is a refreshing surprise for a sweet roll.

BAKE: 375° F. for 20 to 25 minutes   MAKES: 18 rolls

1 loaf frozen white (or sweet) bread dough, thawed
2 tablespoons butter or margarine, melted
⅓ cup sugar
1 tablespoon grated lemon peel

Let dough rise until doubled in size. Roll out on floured surface to 18x10-inch rectangle. Brush with butter. Combine sugar and peel; sprinkle over dough. Roll up, starting with 18-inch side. Cut into 18 pieces. Place, cut-side down, in well-greased 13x9-inch pan. Cover; let rise in warm place until light or doubled in size, 30 to 60 minutes.

Bake at 375° F. for 20 to 25 minutes, or until light golden brown. Immediately turn out of pan. Frost warm rolls with Lemon Icing, page 118.

MINCEMEAT ROLLS

A good way to use that extra cup of mincemeat that may be around during the holiday season.

BAKE: 375° F. for 25 to 30 minutes   MAKES: 15 or 16 rolls

1 loaf frozen white (or sweet) bread dough, thawed
1 cup prepared mincemeat

Let dough rise until doubled in size. Roll out on floured surface to a 16x10-inch rectangle. Spread with mincemeat. Roll up, starting with 16-inch side. Cut into 15 or 16 pieces. Place, cut-side down, in well-greased 9x9- or 10x8-inch pan. Cover; let rise in warm place until light or doubled in size, 30 to 60 minutes.

Bake at 375° F. for 25 to 30 minutes. Remove from pan. Frost warm rolls with Butterscotch Icing, page 118. If desired, garnish with red candied cherries.

SUGGESTION: One chopped, pared apple may be added to the mincemeat.

DANISH COFFEE ROLLS

Youngsters will like these rolls—they look just like the ones you buy in a bake shop.

BAKE: 375° F. for 15 to 20 minutes   MAKES: 12 rolls

1 loaf frozen white (or sweet) bread dough, thawed
1 tablespoon butter or margarine, melted
½ Sugar Streusel recipe, page 121
1 tablespoon beaten egg
2 teaspoons milk
jam, jelly, or fruit pie filling

Let dough rise until almost doubled in size. Roll out on floured surface to 12-inch square. Brush with butter; then cut into 1-inch strips. Twist each strip many times and coil onto greased cookie sheet, keeping flat. Cover; let rise in warm place until light or doubled in size, 30 to 60 minutes.

Combine egg and milk. Brush carefully over rolls. Sprinkle each with a teaspoonful of Streusel. Bake at 375° F. for 15 minutes. Place a spoonful of jam in center of each. Bake 3 to 5 minutes. Frost with an icing, page 118, if desired.

DANISH "S" ROLLS:
Twist strips from above recipe; place in "S" shape, with sides touching, on greased cookie sheet. Let rise, brush with egg mixture, sprinkle with Streusel, and place lemon pie filling or jelly along center strip. Bake and frost.

GOLDEN ORANGE CURLICUES

Pretty rolls have a double orange flavor—on the inside and on top.

BAKE: 375° F. for 15 to 20 minutes   MAKES: 15 rolls

1 loaf frozen white (or sweet) bread dough, thawed
2 tablespoons butter or margarine
2 tablespoons flour
2 tablespoons orange juice
1 tablespoon grated orange peel
1 cup powdered sugar

Let dough rise until doubled in size. Melt butter in small saucepan; stir in flour and juice. Cook until thickened. Stir in peel and powdered sugar. Roll out dough on floured surface to 15x12-inch rectangle. Spread a thin layer of orange mixture lengthwise over half the dough. Fold uncovered dough over filling. Cut into 1-inch strips. Twist each strip 4 times and coil onto foil-lined and greased cookie sheet, tucking end under. Cover; let rise in warm place until light or doubled in size, 30 to 60 minutes.

Bake at 375° F. for 15 to 20 minutes. Top each roll with jelly, if desired. Frost warm rolls with remaining orange mixture.

DANISH CURLICUES:
Substitute the following almond mixture for the orange in the above rolls: Beat a small egg slightly. Combine 1 cup *almonds*, ground, 1 cup *powdered sugar*, all but 1 tablespoon of the egg, 1 to 3 tablespoons *water*, and ½ teaspoon *almond extract*, until of a spreading consistency. Combine remaining egg with 1 teaspoon *water*; brush over shaped rolls. Baked rolls may be frosted with Almond Icing, page 118, if desired.

STREUSEL NUT SQUARES

Crisp cookie rolls are topped with a streusel mixture for an old-fashioned look. A spoonful of jelly or jam adds extra color.

BAKE: 400° F. for 12 to 15 minutes   MAKES: 16 rolls

1 loaf frozen white (or sweet) bread dough, thawed
2 tablespoons butter or margarine, melted
1 recipe Sugar Streusel, page 121
¼ cup chopped pecans

Let dough rise until doubled in size. Roll out on floured surface to a 16-inch square. Brush with butter. Combine Streusel and pecans; sprinkle over dough. Cut into 4-inch squares. Place on greased cookie sheet. Cover; let rise in warm place 30 minutes.

Bake at 400° F. for 12 to 15 minutes. Frost warm rolls with one of the icings on page 118. If desired, top each roll with a spoonful of jelly or jam before baking.

SUGAR CHIP TWISTS

For the youngsters, fill the rolls with chocolate chips. For a breakfast roll or the coffee party, try one of the variations.

BAKE: 375° F. for 15 to 18 minutes   MAKES: 15 rolls

1 loaf frozen white (or sweet) bread dough, thawed
2 tablespoons butter or margarine, melted
¼ cup sugar
½ cup chocolate chips

Let dough rise until doubled in size. Roll out on floured surface to a 15x12-inch rectangle. Brush with butter. Sprinkle with sugar and chips. Fold over one-third of dough along 15-inch side. Fold over other third to make 3 layers. Press down lightly. Cut into 1-inch strips. Twist each strip twice and place on greased cookie sheet. Cover; let rise in warm place until light or doubled in size, 30 to 60 minutes.

Bake at 375° F. for 15 to 18 minutes. If desired, frost warm rolls with Coffee Icing, page 118.

ORANGE TWISTS:
Omit chocolate pieces and add 2 tablespoons grated *orange peel* to the sugar. Frost with Orange Icing, page 118.

WALNUT TWISTS:
Combine in small saucepan 1 cup finely chopped *walnuts* or other nuts, 2 tablespoons *sugar,* 2 tablespoons *honey,* 2 tablespoons *flour,* and ½ cup *half and half cream.* Cook over low heat, stirring constantly, until thick; cool to lukewarm. Substitute for sugar and chips.

DATE TWISTS:
Combine in small saucepan 1 cup halved *dates,* ⅓ cup *orange juice* or water, and 2 tablespoons *sugar.* Cook over low heat, stirring constantly, until thick. Stir in ¼ cup chopped *nuts* and 1 teaspoon grated *orange peel.* Substitute for sugar and chips. Brush hot baked rolls with soft *butter;* sprinkle with *powdered sugar.*

DOUBLE SWEET TWISTS

Butterscotch-flavored graham cracker crumbs are the makeup
of the filling in these double twisted rolls.

BAKE: 375° F. for 12 to 15 minutes   MAKES: 24 rolls

1 loaf frozen white (or sweet) bread dough, thawed
¼ cup butter or margarine, melted
¼ cup brown sugar
½ cup graham cracker crumbs
⅓ cup finely chopped nuts
½ teaspoon cinnamon

Let dough rise until doubled in size. Combine remaining ingredients. Roll out dough on floured surface to a 16x12-inch rectangle. Spread with filling. Roll up each 12-inch side until both sides meet in the center of the rectangle. Cut into ½-inch pieces. Twist each roll to make an "S" shape. Place on well-greased cookie sheets. Cover; let rise in warm place until light, 30 to 60 minutes.

Bake at 375° F. for 12 to 15 minutes. Remove from sheets immediately.

COOKIE BUNS

Tiny sugar-coated rolls take on a cookie look. Ideal with a cup
of coffee or as an after school snack.

BAKE: 375° F. for 12 to 15 minutes   MAKES: 36 tiny rolls

1 loaf frozen white (or sweet) bread dough, thawed
⅓ cup sugar
¼ cup coconut or finely chopped nuts
1 tablespoon brown sugar
1 teaspoon cinnamon
⅓ cup butter or margarine, melted

Divide dough into thirds; then divide each third into 12 pieces. Combine sugars, coconut, and cinnamon. Coat dough pieces first with butter, then with the cinnamon-sugar mixture. Place 1 inch apart on greased cookie sheets. Cover; let rise in warm place until very light or doubled in size, 1 to 1½ hours.

Bake at 375° F. for 12 to 15 minutes. Frost with one of the icings on page 118.

ORANGE OR LEMON COOKIE BUNS:
Omit cinnamon; add 1 to 2 tablespoons grated *orange* or *lemon peel* to sugar mixture. Frost with Orange or Lemon Icing, page 118.

CHERRY STREUSEL TRIANGLES

Cherry jam and the streusel topping give these sweet rolls a Danish look.

BAKE: 375° F. for 15 to 18 minutes   MAKES: 16 rolls

1 loaf frozen white (or sweet) bread dough, thawed
½ cup cherry preserves
1 recipe Sugar Streusel, page 121
1 tablespoon egg
1 tablespoon water

Let dough rise until doubled in size. Roll out on floured surface to a 16x12-inch rectangle. Spread with cherry preserves; then sprinkle with half the Streusel mixture. Fold over one-third of dough along 16-inch side; then fold over the other third to make three layers. Brush top with mixture of egg and water; then sprinkle with remaining Streusel. Cut into 16 triangles about 2 inches on the bottom. Place on greased cookie sheets. Cover; let rise until light, about 30 minutes.

Bake at 375° F. for 15 to 18 minutes. If desired, frost with Vanilla Icing, page 118.

SWEETHEART ROLLS

These rolls take on a heart shape as they rise and bake.

BAKE: 375° F. for 15 to 18 minutes   MAKES: 20 rolls

1 loaf frozen white (or sweet) bread dough, thawed
3 tablespoons butter or margarine, melted
⅓ cup brown sugar
¼ cup bread or graham cracker crumbs
¼ cup finely chopped nuts
1 teaspooon cinnamon

Let dough rise until doubled in size. Roll out on floured surface to a 20x8-inch rectangle. Brush with butter. Combine brown sugar, crumbs, nuts, and cinnamon; sprinkle over dough. Press down firmly. Fold 20-inch sides to center just to meet. Fold sides again as if closing a book. Cut into 1-inch pieces. Place 3 inches apart on cookie sheets that have been lined with foil and then greased. Flatten slightly. Cover; let rise in warm place until light or doubled in size, 30 to 60 minutes.

Bake at 375° F. for 15 to 18 minutes. Frost with Vanilla Icing, page 118.

OPEN-FACED KOLACKIES

Another heritage recipe—from the Bohemians comes this roll filled or topped with prunes. Great as a breakfast roll.

BAKE: 375° F. for 15 to 18 minutes   MAKES: 18 rolls

1 loaf frozen white (sweet or honey wheat) bread dough, thawed
¾ cup cooked prunes or apricots, cut up
2 tablespoons sugar
1 teaspoon grated orange or lemon peel
¼ cup finely chopped nuts, if desired

Let dough rise until doubled in size. Divide into 18 pieces. Combine remaining ingredients. Flatten each piece of dough, shaping into 3-inch round. Place on greased cookie sheets. Cover; let rise in warm place 30 minutes. With floured fingers make a deep impression in centers. Top each with a teaspoonful of prune mixture.

Bake at 375° F. for 15 to 18 minutes. Frost with one of the icings on page 118, or sprinkle with powdered sugar before serving.

OLD-FASHIONED KOLACKIES:
(The filling is enclosed inside these kolackies.) After topping each flattened piece of dough with filling, bring dough around to enclose the filling. Seal well and place 2 inches apart, seam-side down, on greased cookie sheet. Let rise and bake. (Sometimes you may want the filling to peek through: Bring corners of dough to top of filling; pinch together but allow filling to show. Place, seam-side up, on greased cookie sheet.)

DELUXE KOLACKIES:
Combine ⅓ cup (3 oz.) *cream cheese* or well-drained small curd cottage cheese, 2 tablespoons *sugar,* and 1 tablespoon *milk* or cream. Place a half-teaspoon on top of the prune or apricot mixture.

LEMON DROPS

Lemon sugar adds a refreshing touch to a simple sweet roll.

BAKE: 375° F. for 15 to 18 minutes   MAKES: 12 large or 18 medium rolls

1 loaf frozen white (or sweet) bread dough, thawed
¼ cup sugar
1 tablespoon grated lemon or orange peel
⅛ teaspoon nutmeg
2 tablespoons butter or margarine, melted

Divide dough into 12 to 18 pieces. Shape into balls. Combine sugar, peel, and nutmeg. Dip tops of rolls first into butter and then into sugar mixture. Place, sugared-side up, in greased muffin cups. With scissors, cut a cross on top of rolls about ½-inch deep. Cover; let rise in warm place until light or doubled in size, 1 to 1½ hours.

Bake at 375° F. for 15 to 18 minutes. Remove from pan immediately.

APPLE PASTRIES

Just like little pies are these foldovers filled with fruit pie filling.
They make a good dessert for a picnic or camping trip.

BAKE: 400° F. for 15 to 18 minutes   MAKES: 12

1 loaf frozen white (or sweet) bread dough, thawed
1 can prepared apple, cherry, blueberry, or other fruit pie filling
soft butter
powdered sugar

Let dough rise until doubled in size. Divide into 12 pieces. Flatten and roll out each piece to a 6-inch circle. Top with 2 tablespoons filling. Moisten edge and fold in half; seal well. Transfer to well-greased cookie sheet. With scissors, snip a short gash on top of each. Cover; let rise in warm place 30 minutes.

Bake at 400° F. for 15 to 18 minutes. While hot, brush with butter and sprinkle with powdered sugar. Best the first day.

TIP: Use mostly fruit for filling. If too much of the sauce is used, it will run out onto cookie sheet.

NUTTY COOKIE ROLLS

Small rolls that make a good cookie—especially when some-
thing not too sweet is desired.

BAKE: 375° F. for 15 to 18 minutes   MAKES: 36 small rolls

1 loaf frozen white (or sweet) bread dough, thawed
3 tablespoons sugar
jam or preserves
¼ cup finely chopped nuts
1 tablespoon butter or margarine, melted

Let dough rise until doubled in size. Roll out on floured surface to a 12-inch square; sprinkle with half the sugar. Fold over and roll out again. Cut into 2-inch squares. Place a half-teaspoon jam on each square. Moisten edges, fold over, and seal. Combine remaining sugar with nuts. Brush tops of rolls with butter; dip into sugar mixture. Place on greased cookie sheets. Cover; let rise in warm place until light, about 30 minutes.

Bake at 375° F. for 15 to 18 minutes.

CHERRY CHIP COOKIE ROLLS:
Combine ⅓ cup (3 oz.) *cream cheese,* ¼ cup *sugar,* and ½ slightly beaten egg. Add ½ cup *chocolate chips* and ¼ cup cut *maraschino cherries.* Substitute for jam and place 1 teaspoon on each square.

JAM WHIRLS

Petite sweet rolls with whirl of jam in the middle and a crunchy coating of cinnamon sugar on the outside.

BAKE: 375° F. for 12 to 15 minutes   MAKES: 18 rolls

1 loaf frozen white (or sweet) bread dough, thawed
⅓ cup fruit preserves, any flavor
2 tablespoons bread or graham cracker crumbs
1 tablespoon butter or margarine, melted
2 tablespoons Cinnamon Sugar, page 121

Let dough rise until doubled in size. Roll out on floured surface to an 18x10-inch rectangle. Brush with preserves*; sprinkle with crumbs. Cut into two 18x5-inch rectangles. Roll up, starting with 18-inch side. Brush tops with butter; sprinkle with cinnamon sugar. Cut into 2-inch pieces. Place, seam-side down, on greased cookie sheet. With dull side of table knife, press a deep crease across center top of each roll. Cover; let rise in warm place until light or doubled in size, 30 to 60 minutes.

Press down center top of each roll again. Bake at 375° F. for 12 to 15 minutes.

*Spread jam to within ½ inch of the 18-inch sides. When rolling up strip, start with the inside cut edge and roll toward the uncovered edge.

CINNAMON ROLL DOUGHNUTS

Cinnamon rolls fried to look and taste like a doughnut.

DEEP FAT FRY: 365° F. for 2 to 3 minutes   MAKES: 30

2 loaves frozen white (or sweet) bread dough, thawed
1 tablespoon water
1 tablespoon beaten egg
2 tablespoons sugar
2 teaspoons cinnamon

Let dough rise until doubled in size. Roll out each loaf on floured surface to a 15x10-inch rectangle. Brush lightly with mixture of water and egg. Combine sugar and cinnamon; sprinkle over dough. Roll up, starting with 15-inch side. Cut into 1-inch pieces. Place, cut-side down, on floured cookie sheets. Cover; let rise until very light, 30 to 60 minutes.

Fry in deep hot fat (365° F.) 2 to 3 minutes, turning to brown on both sides. Place on absorbent paper. Roll in sugar or frost with one of the icings on page 118.

LEMON DESSERT ROLLS

A twist of dough forms the ring that holds the pie filling on top of these luscious rolls. A prepared pie filling makes it easy.

BAKE: 375° F. for 15 to 20 minutes   MAKES: 12 to 15 rolls

1 loaf frozen white (or sweet) bread dough, thawed
lemon, cherry, blueberry or other prepared fruit pie filling
powdered sugar

Let dough rise until doubled in size. Roll out on floured surface to ¼-inch thickness. Cut into 2½ to 3-inch rounds. Place on greased cookie sheet. Divide remaining dough into as many pieces as rounds. Moisten edges of rounds. Shape pieces into about 8-inch strips. Seal ends together and place on edge of rounds. Fill centers with 1 tablespoon filling. Cover; let rise in warm place until light, 30 to 60 minutes.

Bake at 375° F. for 15 to 20 minutes, or until bread is golden brown. Frost with Vanilla Icing, page 118, or sprinkle with powdered sugar.

MERINGUE CRESCENTS

A crisp sweet meringue rolled up in these crescents makes interesting sweet rolls.

BAKE: 325° F. for 20 to 25 minutes   MAKES: 32 small rolls

1 loaf frozen white (or sweet) bread dough, thawed
1 egg white
⅓ cup sugar
½ cup finely chopped nuts
½ teaspoon vanilla
butter
powdered sugar

Let dough rise until doubled in size. Beat egg white until soft mounds form. Gradually add sugar; continue beating until very stiff. Fold in nuts and vanilla.

Divide dough into four parts. Roll out one part on floured surface to 9-inch circle; spread with ¼ of the meringue. Cut into 8 wedges. Roll up each wedge, starting at wide end. Place, point-side down, on greased cookie sheets. Repeat with remaining dough. Cover; let rise in warm place 30 minutes.

Bake at 325° F. for 20 to 25 minutes. Brush immediately with soft butter; then sprinkle with powdered sugar.

SUGGESTION: Substitute ½ cup chocolate chips or 2 ounces shaved semi-sweet or sweet baking chocolate for the nuts.

RAISED DOUGHNUTS

An easy way to start making raised doughnuts. Each loaf makes 15 to 18 doughnuts, depending on size and shape. If you don't want to roll and cut dough, just try twists or knots. It's a good idea to make twists and knots from the leftover pieces after cutting round doughnuts.

DEEP FAT FRY: 365° F. for 2 to 3 minutes   MAKES: 30 to 36 doughnuts

2 loaves frozen white (or sweet) bread dough, thawed

Let dough rise until doubled in size. Roll out on floured surface to ¼ -inch thickness. Cut with doughnut cutter. Place on floured cookie sheets. Cover; let rise in warm place until very light, 30 to 45 minutes.

Fry in deep hot fat (365° F.) 2 to 3 minutes, turning to brown both sides. To serve, coat with granulated or powdered sugar or frost with one of the icings on page 118.

VARIATIONS:

BISMARKS: Cut into 3-inch rounds; do not cut out center. Let rise and fry. To serve, cut a slit in side and fill with *jelly*. Roll in *sugar*.

SWEDISH TWISTS: Divide each loaf into 18 pieces. Shape each piece into 9-inch pencil-like strips. Fold in half and twist twice. Let rise and fry.

LONG JOHNS: Roll out each loaf on floured surface to a 16x8-inch rectangle. Cut into 4x2-inch rectangles. Let rise and fry. To serve, split and fill with a cream filling. (Use a pudding or pie filling mix or your favorite recipe.) Frost with one of the icings on page 118.

DOUGHNUT KNOTS: Divide each loaf into 18 pieces. Shape each piece into 7-inch pencil-like strips. Tie loosely into knots. Let rise and fry.

Coffee Cakes

Coffee cake for breakfast, coffee cake for brunch, coffee cake for coffee get-togethers, coffee cakes for dessert for the bridge party or club meeting —there's one for every occasion. And coffee cake answers the question "What can I serve that is just a little different?"

Making a coffee cake is foolproof when the dough is already made for you. Included in this section are old favorites adapted to frozen dough, as well as completely new ideas.

See the Know-How section at the beginning of this book for special tips on baking with frozen bread doughs.

Before starting to make a coffee cake, be sure to let the loaf of dough rise until it is very light and appears more than doubled in size. It is much easier to roll out when it has risen more than double. Do not knead the dough or handle it too much once it has risen, because the gluten will tighten and it will be difficult to roll out. Just lay it on the floured rolling surface and start rolling and stretching to the desired size. Do not over flour the surface. Some brands of frozen dough roll out more easily than others, thus making the shaping into coffee cakes easier. (Some of the recipes require very little shaping and the coffee cake can be made as soon as the dough is thawed. Follow recipe directions. Dough that does not rise before shaping needs a longer rising time after the coffee cake is made.)

To dust rolls or coffee cakes with powdered sugar, place sugar in a small sieve and press through with finger or spoon. This eliminates lumps and lets you dust evenly.

When coffee cakes are baked on cookie sheets, line sheets with foil and then grease. This will simplify the cleanup.

Coffee Cakes:
1. Cinnamon Roll Loaf
2. Butterscotch Coffee Cake
3. Deluxe Cinnamon Round
4. Easter Rabbit Coffee Cake
5. Butterscotch Crown
6. Cinnamon Swirl Braid
7. Easy Danish Kuchen
8. Danish Cream Coffee Cake
9. Swedish Tea Log

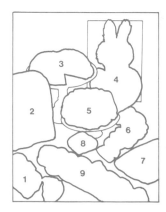

Frozen raisin bread dough, available in many markets, may be used to make many of the coffee cakes. It is especially nice to use in recipes calling for raisins. Also new in a number of areas is a rich, sweet frozen bread dough developed specifically for use in making coffee cakes and sweet rolls. This is good to use in making any of the coffee cake and sweet roll recipes in this book.

CINNAMON ROLL COFFEE CAKES

Cinnamon rolls can be arranged in many ways to take on a special shape for a special day.

BAKE: 375° F. for 20 to 30 minutes   MAKES: 1 or 2 coffee cakes

1 loaf frozen white (or sweet) bread dough, thawed
2 tablespoons butter or margarine, melted
⅓ cup sugar
2 tablespoons graham cracker crumbs, if desired
1 tablespoon brown sugar
1 teaspoon cinnamon

Let dough rise until doubled in size. Roll out on floured surface to a 16x12-inch rectangle. Brush with butter. Combine remaining ingredients; sprinkle all but about 1 tablespoon over dough. Roll up, starting with 16-inch side. Cut into 16 rolls and arrange as directed below. (Flatten rolls slightly before shaping into coffee cake.) Cover; let rise in warm place until light or doubled in size, 30 to 60 minutes. Sprinkle with remaining sugar mixture.

Bake at 375° F. for 20 to 30 minutes. Frost with one of the icings on page 118 and decorate with nuts and cherries as desired.

VARIATIONS:

CHRISTMAS TREE:
Line large cookie sheet with foil; grease. About 3 inches from bottom make a row of 5 cinnamon rolls, overlapping each about ¼ inch. Make next row with 4 rolls, again overlapping onto each other. Continue making rows of 3, 2, and 1. Use 1 roll for the trunk.

CINNAMON LOGS OR CRESCENTS:
Line cookie sheet with foil; grease. Arrange 8 rolls in a log or crescent, overlapping about ½ inch on previous rolls.

CINNAMON RINGS:
Arrange 8 rolls around the edge of greased 8-inch round pan, overlapping slightly. (Rolls may also be arranged in a heart-shaped pan.)

SWEDISH TEA LOG

A variation in the shape of the tea ring—bake it as a log or as a crescent. Any of the fillings for the Swedish Tea Ring, page 96, can be used in the log.

BAKE: 375° F. for 20 to 25 minutes   MAKES: 15-inch log

1 loaf frozen white (or sweet) bread dough, thawed
2 tablespoons butter or margarine, melted
¼ cup brown sugar
1 teaspoon cinnamon
¼ cup chopped nuts

Let dough rise until doubled in size. Roll out on lightly floured surface to a 15x12-inch rectangle. Brush with butter. Sprinkle with a mixture of the sugar, cinnamon, and nuts. Roll up, starting with 15-inch side. Place diagonally as a log or crescent on a cookie sheet that has been lined with foil and then greased. Starting at top, make cuts through the roll ¾ inch apart and to within ½ inch of bottom. Bring slices to sides of log, alternating sides, and turning each on a cut side. Cover; let rise in warm place until light or doubled in size, 30 to 60 minutes.

Bake at 375° F. for 20 to 25 minutes. Frost warm log with Vanilla Icing, page 118.

CUPID'S COFFEE CAKE

An easy shaping idea results in a heart-shaped cake—no special pans needed.

BAKE: 350° F. for 25 to 30 minutes   MAKES: 2 hearts

1 loaf frozen white (or sweet) bread dough, thawed
2 tablespoons butter or margarine, melted
⅓ cup sugar
1 teaspoon cinnamon
¼ cup chopped nuts or coconut, if desired

Let dough rise until doubled in size. Roll out on floured surface to a 20x8-inch rectangle. Brush with butter. Combine sugar, cinnamon, and nuts; sprinkle over dough. Roll up, starting with 20-inch side. Seal seam. Cut in half to make two 10-inch pieces. Place one roll on greased cookie sheet. Fold this roll in half; seal ends together. Starting at folded end, cut with scissors down center of roll to within 1 inch of other end. Turn cut halves flat on side, cut-side up, to make heart shape. Repeat with remaining dough. Cover; let rise in warm place until light or doubled in size, 30 to 60 minutes.

Bake at 350° F. for 25 to 30 minutes. If desired, spoon about 2 tablespoons red jelly onto each heart and bake 5 minutes. Frost with Vanilla Icing, page 118.

NOTE: One large heart may be made. Be sure to use a large cookie sheet.

DELUXE CINNAMON ROUND

Coffee cake bread is layered with cinnamon sugar and raisins.

BAKE: 350° F. for 30 to 35 minutes   MAKES: 1 round loaf

1 loaf frozen white (or sweet) bread dough, thawed
½ cup sugar
1 teaspoon cinnamon
½ cup raisins
1 tablespoon butter or margarine, melted

Let dough rise until doubled in size. Divide into fourths. Roll out each piece on floured surface to an 8-inch circle. Place first circle in well-greased 9-inch round pan. Combine sugar and cinnamon; sprinkle 2 tablespoons over dough; then top with a third of the raisins. Top with a second circle of dough; sprinkle with cinnamon sugar and raisins. Repeat with remaining dough. Press down firmly when topped with the fourth round of dough; brush with butter and sprinkle with remaining cinnamon sugar. Cover; let rise in warm place until light or doubled in size, 30 to 60 minutes.

Bake at 350° F. for 30 to 35 minutes. Remove from pan immediately.

CINNAMON ROLL LOAF

Cinnamon raisin rolls make up these little sweet loaves.

BAKE: 375° F. for 25 to 30 minutes   MAKES: 2 small loaves

1 loaf frozen white (or sweet) bread dough, thawed
¼ cup butter or margarine, melted
⅓ cup sugar (half brown)
1½ teaspoons cinnamon
½ cup raisins

Let dough rise until doubled in size. Roll out on floured surface to a 16x10-inch rectangle. Brush with most of the butter. Combine sugars and cinnamon; sprinkle all but 1 tablespoon over dough. Sprinkle with raisins. Roll up, starting with 16-inch side. Cut into 16 pieces. Stand 8 rolls, seam-side down, in greased 8x4-inch pan. Repeat with remaining rolls in a second 8x4-inch pan. Brush tops with remaining butter. Sprinkle loaves with remaining cinnamon sugar. Cover; let rise in warm place until light or doubled in size, 30 to 60 minutes.

Bake at 375° F. for 25 to 30 minutes. Cool 1 minute before removing from pan. Frost with Vanilla Icing, page 118, if desired.

MONKEY BREAD

One of the old, old favorites in coffee cakes—bubbles of bread
are coated with sugar-cinnamon mixture.

BAKE: 350° F. for 35 to 40 minutes   MAKES: 1 coffee cake

1 loaf frozen white (or sweet) bread dough, thawed
½ cup sugar (half brown)
1 teaspoon cinnamon
½ cup coconut or chopped nuts, if desired
¼ cup butter or margarine, melted

Cut dough into 24 small pieces. Combine sugar, cinnamon, and coconut. Coat dough pieces with butter; then roll in sugar mixture. Place in well-greased 9- or 12-cup bundt pan. Cover; let rise in warm place until light or doubled in size, 1½ to 2 hours.

Bake at 350° F. for 35 to 40 minutes. Cool for 1 or 2 minutes; then loosen edges and carefully turn out onto serving plate.

NOTE: Bread may be baked in 2 bread loaf pans or a tube pan with a solid bottom.

ORANGE-COCONUT BUBBLE LOAF:
Substitute 2 tablespoons grated *orange peel* for the cinnamon.

CINNAMON SWIRL BRAID

Cinnamon, sugar, and raisins go into this braid. Any of the
fillings for the Swedish Tea Ring can be used.

BAKE: 350° F. for 25 to 30 minutes   MAKES: 15-inch braid

1 loaf frozen white (or sweet) bread dough, thawed
1½ tablespoons butter or margarine, melted
⅓ cup sugar
⅓ cup raisins
1 teaspoon cinnamon

Let dough rise until doubled in size. Roll out on floured surface to a 14-inch square. Brush with most of the butter. Combine sugar, raisins, and cinnamon; sprinkle most over the dough. Cut into 3 strips; roll up each, starting with 14-inch side. Seal seams. Braid together. Place on greased cookie sheet, curving slightly for crescent shape. Brush with remaining butter and sprinkle with remaining cinnamon sugar. Cover; let rise in warm place until light, 30 to 60 minutes.

Bake at 350° F. for 25 to 30 minutes.

SWEET BRAID

Each strip has its own swirl of filling.

BAKE: 375° F. for 25 to 30 minutes   MAKES: 1 coffee cake

1 loaf frozen white (or sweet) bread dough, thawed
½ cup raisins
½ cup chopped or sliced almonds
2 tablespoons sugar
2 tablespoons grated orange peel

Let dough rise until doubled in size. Roll out on floured surface to a 14-inch square. Sprinkle with raisins, almonds, sugar, and peel; press down firmly. Cut into 3 strips; roll up each lengthwise, sealing seams well. Braid the three strips together. Place on greased cookie sheet, curving slightly for crescent shape. Cover; let rise in warm place until light or doubled in size, 30 to 60 minutes.

Bake at 375° F. for 25 to 30 minutes. If desired, frost warm coffee cake with Orange Icing, page 118.

BUTTERSCOTCH CROWN

Raisin-filled butterscotch rolls baked in a bundt pan result in a coffee cake glistening with goodness.

BAKE: 350° F. for 35 to 40 minutes   MAKES: 1 coffee cake ring

1 loaf frozen white (or sweet) bread dough, thawed
2 tablespoons butter or margarine, melted
¼ cup brown sugar
½ teaspoon cinnamon
⅓ cup raisins

Let dough rise until doubled in size. Roll out on floured surface to an 18x10-inch rectangle. Brush with butter; sprinkle with remaining ingredients. Roll up, starting with 18-inch side. Cut into 18 rolls. Place, cut-side down, in well-greased 9- or 12-cup bundt pan in two layers. Cover; let rise in warm place until light or doubled in size, 30 to 60 minutes.

Bake at 350° F. for 35 to 40 minutes. Cool 1 or 2 minutes. Turn out onto rack covered with waxed paper.

CHRISTMAS CROWN:
Sprinkle ½ cup mixed *candied fruit* or candied cherries, halved, over filling before rolling up. Frost baked crown with half a recipe of Vanilla Icing, page 118.

EASY DANISH KUCHEN

An easy coffee cake for the beginner, this fruit topped coffee cake offers both eye appeal and good eating.

BAKE: 375° F. for 20 to 25 minutes   MAKES: 2 coffee cakes

1 loaf frozen white (or sweet) bread dough, thawed
2 tablespoons butter or margarine, melted
1 cup prepared fruit pie filling or preserves
1 recipe Sugar Streusel, page 121

Let dough rise until doubled in size. Divide in half. Roll out, half at a time, on floured surface to a 12x10-inch rectangle. Brush with half the butter and spread half the filling to within 1 inch of all edges. Fold up about ½ inch of dough on each end; then fold over about 2 inches on each side, leaving an opening down the center. Place on greased cookie sheets. Sprinkle Sugar Streusel over the tops. Cover; let rise in warm place until light or doubled in size, 30 to 60 minutes.

Bake at 375° F. for 20 to 25 minutes. Frost warm coffee cakes with one of the icings on page 118, if desired.

ORANGE TWIST COFFEE CAKE

Coconut is twisted up in rolls that sparkle with an orange glaze.

BAKE: 375° F. for 20 to 25 minutes   MAKES: 13x9-inch coffee cake

1 loaf frozen white (or sweet) bread dough, thawed
2 tablespoons butter or margarine, melted
½ cup coconut
2 tablespoons sugar
1 tablespoon grated orange peel
½ cup powdered sugar

Let dough rise until doubled in size. Roll out on floured surface to a 15x10-inch rectangle. Brush with butter. Combine coconut, sugar, and peel; sprinkle over dough. Fold in half lengthwise. Cut into 1-inch strips. Twist strips 2 or 3 times and place in 3 rows in well-greased 13x9-inch pan. Cover; let rise in warm place until light, 30 to 60 minutes.

Bake at 375° F. for 20 to 25 minutes, or until light golden brown. Brush with half the Orange Glaze; bake 5 minutes. Cool slightly and add powdered sugar to remaining glaze and spread over rolls.

ORANGE GLAZE:
Combine in small saucepan ⅓ cup *sugar*, 2 tablespoons *orange juice*, and 2 tablespoons *butter* or margarine. Boil 2 minutes. Stir in 1 teaspoon grated *orange peel*.

BUTTERSCOTCH NUT LOAF

Swirls of butterscotch nut filling in between thin layers of bread.
Keep in refrigerator for a quick coffee snack.

BAKE: 350° F. for 30 to 35 minutes   MAKES: 2 loaves

1 loaf frozen white (or sweet) bread dough, thawed
1 cup packed brown sugar
1 cup finely chopped nuts
1 teaspoon cinnamon
2 tablespoons butter or margarine, melted
1 tablespoon water

Let dough rise until almost doubled in size. Divide in half. Roll out, half at a time, on floured surface to a 14x6-inch rectangle. Combine brown sugar with remaining ingredients. Spread half over dough to within ½ inch of edges. Moisten edges; roll up, starting with 6-inch side, and seal seams well. Place in well-greased 8x4- or 9x5-inch pan. Cover; let rise in warm place until light or doubled in size, about 1 hour.

Bake at 350° F. for 30 to 35 minutes. To serve, cut into thin slices.

BUTTERSCOTCH SNOWBALLS

Little balls smothered with a butterscotch sauce and coconut
make up the big snowball.

BAKE: 375° F. for 20 to 25 minutes   MAKES: 2 (8-inch) coffee cakes

1 loaf frozen white (or sweet) bread dough, thawed
¼ cup butter or margarine
½ cup brown sugar
2 tablespoons milk
1 cup coconut

Divide dough in half; then divide each half into 20 pieces. Shape into balls. Place in 2 well-greased 8-inch round cake or pie pans (20 rolls per pan). Cover; let rise in warm place until light, 1 to 1½ hours.

Bake at 375° F. for 15 to 20 minutes, or until light golden brown. Meanwhile combine butter, brown sugar, and milk in small saucepan and bring to a boil, stirring constantly. Brush over coffee cakes and sprinkle with coconut. Bake 5 minutes. Remove from pans immediately.

FROSTY SNOWBALL CAKES

So simple! Tiny balls frosted while warm and sprinkled with nuts add a sweet touch.

BAKE: 350° F. for 25 to 30 minutes   MAKES: 2 (8-inch) coffee cakes

1 loaf frozen white (or sweet) bread dough, thawed
icing, page 118 (preferably fruit-flavored, rum, or maple)
chopped nuts or coconut

Divide dough into 30 pieces. Shape into balls. Place in 2 greased 9-inch pie pans or 8-inch round cake pans (15 balls per pan). Cover; let rise in warm place until light or doubled in size, 1½ to 2 hours.

Bake at 350° F. for 25 to 30 minutes. Remove from pans. Frost warm cakes with half the icing. Cool; frost with remaining icing. Sprinkle with nuts.

SPLIT TWIRL LOAF

An unusual shaping makes this a unique loaf.

BAKE: 350° F. for 25 to 30 minutes   MAKES: 2 small loaves

1 loaf frozen white (or sweet) bread dough, thawed
1 cup cut prunes or other dried fruits
⅓ cup water or orange juice
2 tablespoons sugar
1 teaspoon grated lemon or orange peel, if desired
2 tablespoons Cinnamon Sugar, page 121

Let dough rise until doubled in size. Cook prunes with water and sugar until tender. Stir in peel. Cool to warm. Roll out dough on floured surface to a 16x10-inch rectangle. Spread with filling. Roll up, starting with 16-inch side. Cut in half lengthwise, making two 16-inch strips. Fold each in half, keeping cut-side up and parallel. Place each, cut-side up, in a well-greased 8x4-inch (or slightly smaller) pan. Cover; let rise in warm place until light or doubled in size, 30 to 60 minutes.

Sprinkle cinnamon sugar on tops. Bake at 350° F. for 25 to 30 minutes. Remove from pans immediately. If desired, frost with one of the icings on page 118.

SUGGESTION: Substitute for the prune filling any of the fillings from the Swedish Tea Ring recipe, page 96, or use one (12-oz.) can of cake and pastry filling.

APPLE KUCHEN

A coffee cake that comes to us from Germany. Apple is the most common topping, but try it with other fresh fruit.

BAKE: 350° F. for 35 to 40 minutes   MAKES: 13x9-inch coffee cake

1 loaf frozen white (or sweet) bread dough, thawed
2 cups thinly sliced, pared apples
2 tablespoons butter or margarine
½ cup sugar
1 teaspoon cinnamon
1 egg
¼ cup cream

Let dough rise slightly. Press into well-greased 13x9-inch pan. Arrange apples on top. Cut butter into sugar and cinnamon. Sprinkle over apples. Cover; let rise in warm place until doubled in size, 1 to 1½ hours.

Bake at 350° F. for 20 to 25 minutes, or until light golden brown. Beat egg and cream together until blended. Spoon over apples. Bake 10 to 15 minutes or until custard is set and apples are tender. Best the day baked. Refrigerate leftover coffee cake. Reheat to serve.

MORE IDEAS (Substitute one of the following for the apples):

PLUM OR APRICOT KUCHEN: Use 12 fresh Italian plums, prunes, or apricots, halved.

PEACH KUCHEN: Use 2 cups sliced fresh peaches.

BLUEBERRY OR RASPBERRY KUCHEN: Use 1 or 2 cups fresh or frozen blueberries or raspberries.

RHUBARB KUCHEN: Use 2 cups fresh or frozen sliced rhubarb.

QUICKIE ORANGE COFFEE CAKE

Bubbles of bread are crunchy with orange sugar and gooey on the bottom.

BAKE: 375° F. for 20 to 25 minutes   MAKES: 13x9-inch coffee cake

1 loaf frozen white (or sweet) bread dough, thawed
¼ cup butter or margarine, melted
¼ cup orange juice
1 tablespoon grated orange peel
⅓ cup sugar

Cut dough into 36 pieces; place in well-buttered 13x9-inch pan. Combine butter and orange juice; spoon over dough pieces. Mix together peel and sugar; sprinkle over all. Cover; let rise in warm place until very light and more than doubled in size, 1 to 1½ hours.

Bake at 375° F. for 20 to 25 minutes. Immediately loosen edges and turn out on rack lined with waxed paper. Best warm.

STREUSEL COFFEE CAKE

Your choice of some old ethnic coffee cakes. Easy to have on hand for a coffee treat.

BAKE: 375° F. for 20 to 25 minutes   MAKES: 13x9-inch coffee cake

1 loaf frozen white (or sweet) bread dough, thawed
½ cup sugar
¾ cup flour
¼ cup butter or margarine
½ teaspoon cinnamon

When dough is partially risen, press into well-greased 13x9-inch pan. Cut butter into remaining ingredients; sprinkle over dough. Cover; let rise in warm place until doubled in size, 45 to 60 minutes.

Bake at 375° F. for 20 to 25 minutes. Frost with Vanilla Icing, page 118.

MORE IDEAS (Omit topping in above recipe and substitute one of the suggestions below):

DUTCH SUGAR CAKE: Press dough into pan as directed. Let rise. Cut 2 tablespoons *butter* or margarine into ¼ cup *brown sugar*, ¼ cup *sugar*, ¼ cup *flour*, and 1 teaspoon *cinnamon*. Sprinkle dough with this mixture just before baking.

DANISH CARAMEL COFFEE CAKE: Press dough into pan as directed. Let rise. Just before baking press deep holes into dough, about 3 inches apart. Melt together ½ cup *brown sugar*, 3 tablespoons *butter* or margarine, 1 tablespoon *water*, and 2 tablespoons *flour*. Pour over top. Bake.

ORANGE STREUSEL COFFEE CAKE: Combine ½ cup *sugar*, 2 tablespoons *flour*, 2 tablespoons grated *orange peel*, and ½ cup *coconut*; sprinkle over dough. Let rise; just before baking drizzle with a mixture of 2 tablespoons melted *butter* and 2 tablespoons *orange juice*.

SWEDISH CINNAMON COFFEE CAKE: Combine ½ cup *sugar*, 2 tablespoons *butter* or margarine, and 2 teaspoons *cinnamon*. Sprinkle over dough. Let rise and bake.

CHERRY STREUSEL

When you want a coffeetime dessert for about 20 people, this is the one to make.

BAKE: 375° F. for 25 to 30 minutes   MAKES: 15x10-inch coffee cake

1 loaf frozen white (or sweet) bread dough, thawed
1 can (1 lb. 4 oz.) cherry pie filling
¼ cup sugar
¼ cup butter or margarine
1 cup flour

Let dough rise until almost doubled in size. Press into greased 15x10-inch pan. Spread cherries over top. Cut butter into sugar and flour; sprinkle over cherries. Cover; let rise in warm place until doubled in size, 1 to 1½ hours.

Bake at 375° F. for 25 to 30 minutes. Best the first day or reheat to serve.

NOTE: Other prepared pie fillings may be substituted for the cherry.

SWEDISH TOSCA COFFEE CAKE

A favorite sugared almond topping from Sweden glazes this easy coffee cake. Another favorite idea is to split the cake horizontally and fill with a cream filling.

BAKE: 375° F. for 25 to 30 minutes   MAKES: 13x9-inch coffee cake

1 loaf frozen white (or sweet) bread dough, thawed
¼ cup cream
¼ cup butter or margarine
½ cup sugar
2 tablespoons flour
½ cup almond slices
¼ teaspoon almond extract

Let dough rise slightly. Press into well-greased 13x9-inch pan. Combine cream, butter, sugar, flour, and almonds in small saucepan. Bring to boil; boil 2 minutes. Stir in extract. Spoon over dough. Cover; let rise in warm place until doubled in size, 1 to 2 hours.

Bake at 375° F. for 25 to 30 minutes.

DANISH CREAM COFFEE CAKE:
Prepare a package of vanilla cream pie or pudding mix as directed on label. Split and fill the above coffee cake after it has cooled. Refrigerate. (For easier splitting, first cut into two 6½x9-inch rectangles.) Makes a good **coffee party dessert.**

SWEDISH CHURCH BREAD

The original bread made by the Swedish people was mixed and placed in the pan before church. Then the bread was baked for a coffeetime snack when the family returned home. You can do the same thing with this frozen dough recipe.

BAKE: 375° F. for 20 to 25 minutes   MAKES: 13x9-inch coffee cake

1 loaf frozen white (or sweet) bread dough, thawed
½ cup mixed candied fruit
½ cup raisins
¼ cup sugar
2 tablespoons butter or margarine

Let dough rise until doubled in size. Roll out on floured surface to a 18x12-inch rectangle. Cut in half to make 2 (9x12) rectangles. Place one in greased 13x9-inch pan; sprinkle with half the candied fruit and all the raisins. Top with remaining dough; press down firmly. Sprinkle with remaining fruit and sugar. Dot with butter. Cover; let rise in warm place until doubled in size, 30 to 60 minutes.

Bake at 375° F. for 20 to 25 minutes.

TIP: If you want to slow the second rising time, place the dough in the refrigerator. It will take 1 to 1½ hours to rise.

ORANGE ALMOND COFFEE CAKE BARS

Thin bars with a jam topping make an excellent dessert party treat.

BAKE: 375° F. for 20 to 25 minutes   MAKES: 15x10-inch coffee cake

1 loaf frozen white (or sweet) bread dough, thawed
½ cup orange marmalade or apricot preserves
¼ cup sugar
2 tablespoons flour
¼ cup butter or margarine
¼ cup cream
⅔ cup almond slices

Let dough rise until doubled in size. Press into or roll out to fit a well-greased 15x10-inch pan. Spread with marmalade. Combine remaining ingredients in small saucepan; bring to a boil, stirring constantly. Spoon over marmalade. Cover; let rise in warm place until light or doubled in size, 30 to 45 minutes.

Bake at 375° F. for 20 to 25 minutes.

BLUEBERRY FLIP

The fruit filling makes this coffee cake a good idea for a dessert party.

BAKE: 375° F. for 20 to 25 minutes   MAKES: 2 coffee cakes

1 loaf frozen white (or sweet) bread dough, thawed
2 cups fresh or frozen blueberries
¼ cup sugar
2 tablespoons flour
1 tablespoon butter or margarine

Let dough rise until doubled in size. Combine blueberries, sugar, and flour. Roll out half of dough on floured surface to a 12x10-inch rectangle. Place half of blueberry mixture, lengthwise, down center third of dough. Cut dough diagonally at 1-inch intervals, herringbone fashion, and 3 inches long. Alternately fold opposite strips over filling, crossing in center. Seal ends. Place on well-greased cookie sheet. Repeat with remaining dough. Cover; let rise in warm place until light, 30 to 60 minutes.

Bake at 375° F. for 20 to 25 minutes. Frost warm coffee cakes with Vanilla Icing, page 118. Or brush with butter and sprinkle with powdered sugar.

BUTTERSCOTCH BUBBLE LOAF

A favorite coffee cake made with butterscotch pudding mix.

BAKE: 375° F. for 25 to 30 minutes   MAKES: 1 coffee cake

6 tablespoons butter or margarine, melted
10 or 12 maraschino cherries, if desired
½ cup coconut or chopped nuts
1 loaf frozen white bread dough or 1 pound dinner rolls
1 package (3 to 3 ½ oz.) butterscotch pudding and pie filling mix
¼ cup brown sugar
½ teaspoon cinnamon

Generously butter 12-cup bundt pan or 9x9-inch pan. Arrange cherries on bottom. Sprinkle with coconut. Cut partially thawed loaf into 24 pieces (use rolls frozen). Place pieces in pan. Sprinkle with pudding mix, brown sugar and cinnamon. Drizzle with remaining butter. Cover; let rise in warm place until light or doubled in size, 3 to 4 hours.
Bake at 375° F. for 25 to 30 minutes. Let stand 30 to 60 seconds. Turn out onto plate or wire rack which has been lined with waxed paper.

NOTE: Coffee cake may be shaped night before, using frozen rolls or dough thawed only enough to cut into pieces, and refrigerated. Next day, remove and let stand in warm place until light. (Time needed will vary with amount of rising that took place in the refrigerator.)

APPLE TWIRL

An apple pie-like filling is layered in this coffee cake.

BAKE: 350° F. for 30 to 35 minutes   MAKES: 2 (12-inch) coffee cakes

1 loaf frozen white (or sweet) bread dough, thawed
3 cups chopped, pared apples
½ cup raisins
½ cup sugar
2 tablespoons flour
½ teaspoon nutmeg or cinnamon
butter
powdered sugar

Let dough rise until doubled in size. Combine apples with remaining ingredients. Roll out half of dough on floured surface to a 12-inch square. Place one-fourth of filling down center third of dough. Fold an uncovered side over filling; top with another fourth of filling; then fold over other side. Moisten and seal edges. Place on greased cookie sheet. Make several short cuts on top. Repeat with remaining dough. Cover; let rise in warm place until light, 30 to 45 minutes.

Bake at 350° F. for 30 to 35 minutes. Brush warm coffee cakes with butter and sprinkle with powdered sugar.

CHERRY PIE COFFEE CAKE

Ideal after a bridge game or any time dessert is part of the meeting. Any prepared fruit pie filling may be used, including lemon.

BAKE: 375° F. for 25 to 30 minutes   MAKES: 3 (8-inch) coffee cakes

1 loaf frozen white (or sweet) bread dough, thawed
1 can (1 lb. 4 oz.) cherry pie filling

Let dough rise until doubled in size. Divide into thirds. Roll out each to a 10-inch circle on lightly floured surface. Transfer to greased cookie sheet, stretching to 10-inch circle if necessary. With scissors, make 2-inch cuts, ½ inch apart, around edge. Braid 3 together and curl up to form edge, going all the way around. Place about ⅔ cup filling in center of each. Cover; let rise in warm place until light, 30 to 45 minutes.

Bake at 375° F. for 25 to 30 minutes, or until edges are golden brown. Frost with Vanilla Icing, page 118, or serve topped with a spoonful of whipped cream.

MOCK ALMOND TWIST

Bread crumbs substitute for almonds. If desired, use 1 can (12-oz.) almond pastry filling or almond paste. Or use ½ cup ground almonds for ½ cup crumbs.

BAKE: 375° F. for 25 to 30 minutes   MAKES: 2 (8-inch) coffee cakes

1 loaf frozen white (or sweet) bread dough, thawed
1 cup dry bread crumbs
½ cup sugar
1 egg
1 teaspoon almond extract

Let dough rise until doubled in size. Combine remaining ingredients. Roll out half of dough on floured surface to a 14x8-inch rectangle; spread with half the filling. Roll up, starting with 14-inch side. Cut in half lengthwise with scissors or sharp knife. Twist the two strips together, cut-side up. Shape into ring in 8-inch round pan. Repeat with remaining dough. Cover; let rise in warm place until light, 30 to 60 minutes.

Bake at 375° F. for 25 to 30 minutes. Frost warm coffee cakes with Almond Icing, page 118.

TIP: To hold strips together while twisting, insert a few wooden picks into the strips. Remove before rising.

MOCK ALMOND ROLLS:
After rolling up dough, cut each rolled up strip into 9 pieces. Place in well-buttered muffin cups. Let rise and bake 15 to 18 minutes. Frost.

HAWAIIAN RING

Coconut and a touch of orange are wrapped up in the butterscotch filling.

BAKE: 375° F. for 30 to 35 minutes   MAKES: 1 coffee cake

1 loaf frozen white (or sweet) bread dough, thawed
2 tablespoons butter or margarine, melted
¼ cup brown sugar
½ cup coconut
1 teaspoon grated orange peel
sugar

Let dough rise until doubled in size. Roll out on floured surface to a 16x10-inch rectangle. Brush with butter; then sprinkle with a mixture of the brown sugar, coconut, and peel. Roll up, starting with 16-inch side; moisten and seal edges. Coil into well-greased 9-inch round pan, seam-side down. If desired, sprinkle with sugar. Cover; let rise in warm place until light or doubled in size, 30 to 60 minutes.

Bake at 375° F. for 30 to 35 minutes.

APRICOT BABA DESSERT

An adapted version of a French dessert bread—fun to serve for a bridge party dessert when something unusual and not too rich or sweet is desirable.

BAKE: 350° F. for 30 to 35 minutes

MAKES: 1 bundt dessert (10 to 12 servings)

1 loaf frozen white (or sweet) bread dough, thawed
¼ cup soft butter or margarine
¼ cup white raisins
¼ cup currants
2 tablespoons sugar

Let dough rise until doubled in size. Roll out on floured surface to a 16x12-inch rectangle. Brush with half the butter; sprinkle with fruit and sugar. Roll up, starting with 16-inch side. Cut into 16 pieces. Brush 9- or 12-cup bundt pan with remaining butter. Place rolls, cut-side down, in two layers in pan. Cover; let rise in warm place until very light or doubled in size, 30 to 60 minutes.

Bake at 350° F. for 30 to 35 minutes. Turn out immediately onto serving plate with sides. Spoon hot Apricot Syrup over dessert. Let stand to absorb syrup, spooning over several times. Best served slightly warm; spoon extra syrup over slices.

APRICOT SYRUP:
Combine in saucepan 1 cup *apricot nectar* or juice, ⅓ cup *sugar,* and 1 table-spoon *butter.* Simmer 10 minutes. Stir in 1 tablespoon *lemon juice.*

APRICOT BLOSSOM

Coffee cake rings are filled with apricot preserves and coconut.

BAKE: 375° F. for 25 to 30 minutes   MAKES: 2 small coffee cakes

1 loaf frozen white (or sweet) bread dough, thawed
2 tablespoons butter or margarine, melted
½ cup apricot preserves
1 cup coconut

Let dough rise until doubled in size. Roll out on floured surface to a 20x10-inch rectangle. Brush with butter; then spread with preserves. Sprinkle with coconut. Roll up, starting with 20-inch side. Cut in half to make two 10-inch rolls. Form into rings, sealing ends together. Place in greased 8-inch round pans. Make 5 or 6 cuts across top of each. If desired, brush tops with melted butter and sprinkle with Sugar Streusel, page 121. Cover; let rise until light and doubled in size, 30 to 60 minutes.

Bake at 375° F. for 25 to 30 minutes. If desired, frost with one of the icings on page 118.

JELLY SPLITS

An easy, not too sweet, coffee cake—takes only a split second to shape.

BAKE: 375° F. for 15 to 20 minutes   MAKES: 4 small coffee cakes

1 loaf frozen white (or sweet) bread dough, thawed
1 cup jelly, jam, or fruit pie filling (including lemon)

Let dough rise until doubled in size. Roll out on floured surface to a 14x12-inch rectangle. Cut lengthwise into four 14x3-inch strips. Place strips 2 inches apart on greased cookie sheets. Carefully spoon 2 tablespoons jelly down center of each. Cover; let rise until doubled in size, 30 to 60 minutes.

Bake at 375° F. for 15 to 20 minutes. Spoon remaining jelly down centers; bake 2 or 3 minutes. Frost warm coffee cakes with one of the icings on page 118.

SHAPING VARIATION:
This is a method of shaping that will give a slightly different coffee cake. Instead of being flat and crispy, it will be soft and puffy. Divide dough into 4 parts; shape each into a 14-inch strip. Place 3 inches apart on greased cookie sheets. Let rise until very light. With thumb, make deep depression down centers to within ½ inch from each end. Fill each with 2 tablespoons jelly. Bake· and frost.

COCONUT SWIRL

Coconut in a butterscotch sauce blossoms out on top of this coffee cake.

BAKE: 375° F. for 25 to 30 minutes   MAKES: 1 large coffee cake

1 loaf frozen white (or sweet) bread dough, thawed
2 tablespoons butter or margarine, melted
¼ cup apricot or peach preserves
¼ cup brown sugar
1 cup coconut
½ teaspoon cinnamon

Let dough rise until doubled in size. Roll out on floured surface to an 18x10-inch rectangle. Brush with butter; then spread with preserves. Combine brown sugar, coconut, and cinnamon; sprinkle over dough. Roll up, starting with 18-inch side. Cut in half lengthwise to make two 18-inch strips. Starting in center, loosely coil strip, cut-side up, in pan, pinwheel fashion. Join second strip to end of first. Continue winding to make a flat coffee cake. Cover; let rise in warm place until light or doubled in size, 30 to 60 minutes.

Bake at 375° F. for 25 to 30 minutes. Frost warm coffee cake with Vanilla Icing or Browned Butter Icing, page 118.

BUTTERSCOTCH COFFEE CAKE

Butterscotch pudding mix flavors this coffee cake.

BAKE: 375° F. for 25 to 30 minutes   MAKES: 1 coffee cake

1 loaf frozen white (or sweet) bread dough, thawed
¼ cup butter or margarine, melted
1 package butterscotch pudding and pie filling mix
½ cup coconut or chopped nuts

Let dough rise until doubled in size. Roll out on floured surface to a 16x10-inch rectangle. Brush with butter; then sprinkle with pudding mix and coconut. Roll up, starting with 16-inch side. Form into "U" shape; place in greased 9x9- or 10x8-inch pan. With scissors, make cut halfway through center top the entire "U" shape. Cover; let rise in warm place until light or doubled in size, 30 to 60 minutes.

Bake at 375° F. for 25 to 30 minutes. Remove from pan carefully. Frost warm coffee cake with Vanilla Icing, page 118.

EASTER RABBIT COFFEE CAKE

What fun for the youngsters—a great big Easter Bunny bread.
They'll love it with their eggs for breakfast.

BAKE: 350° F. for 25 to 30 minutes   MAKES: 1 large Easter rabbit

1 loaf frozen white (sweet or raisin) bread dough, thawed
melted butter
2 tablespoons Cinnamon Sugar, page 121
Vanilla Icing, page 118
coconut, if desired
small gum drops and colored tooth picks

Let dough rise until almost doubled in size. Cut off one-third of loaf. From remaining two-thirds, cut off two pieces the size of walnuts. Shape larger piece into a 24-inch strip. Coil onto greased cookie sheet, leaving about 3 inches at bottom of sheet. Shape the third of dough into a 15-inch strip. Twist into flat coil and place on cookie sheet so it just touches first coil. Shape small pieces into 4-inch strips; place at top of smaller coil for "ears."

Brush rabbit generously with butter; sprinkle with cinnamon sugar. Cover; let rise in warm place until doubled in size, 30 to 45 minutes.

Bake at 350° F. for 25 to 30 minutes. Cool and frost. Sprinkle with coconut and make a rabbit face with gumdrops and colored tooth picks.

EASTER BREAKFAST COFFEE CAKE

Serve this beautiful braid for Easter breakfast or brunch. Fill center with plain or colored hard-cooked eggs, or use Easter egg candy.

BAKE: 350° F. for 35 to 40 minutes   MAKES: 15-inch coffee cake ring

2 loaves frozen white (sweet or raisin) bread dough, thawed
1 tablespoon grated orange peel
2 tablespoons of orange juice
2 tablespoons soft butter or margarine
1 cup powdered sugar
coconut

Let bread dough rise until almost doubled in size. Combine the 2 loaves and then divide into thirds. Shape and stretch each third into 20-inch strip. Braid together; shape into ring on large greased cookie sheet. Seal ends together. Cover; let rise in warm place until light or doubled in size, 45 to 60 minutes.

Combine peel, juice, butter, and ½ cup powdered sugar. Brush about one-fourth of this mixture carefully over risen coffee cake. Bake at 350° F. for 25 minutes. Brush with another fourth of the glaze; then bake 10 to 15 minutes. Add ½ cup powdered sugar to remaining glaze and frost warm bread. Sprinkle with coconut. To serve, place on large plate and fill center with cooked eggs or candy eggs.

PINEAPPLE UPSIDE DOWN CAKE

Pineapple in brown sugar glazes the bottom of these rolls— just like an upside down cake.

BAKE: 375° F. for 25 to 30 minutes   MAKES: 15 or 16 rolls

1 loaf frozen white (or sweet) bread dough, thawed
3 tablespoons soft or melted butter or margarine
6 tablespoons brown sugar
¾ cup well-drained crushed pineapple

Let dough rise until doubled in size. Brush 10x8- or 9x9-inch pan with 2 tablespoons butter. Sprinkle with ¼ cup brown sugar and pineapple. Roll out dough on floured surface to a 15x12-inch rectangle. Brush with remaining butter; sprinkle with 2 tablespoons brown sugar and cinnamon. Roll up, starting with 15-inch side. Cut into 15 or 16 pieces. Place, cut-side down, in prepared pan. Cover; let rise in warm place until light or doubled in size, 30 to 60 minutes.

Bake at 375° F. for 25 to 30 minutes. Cool 1 minute, then turn out onto wire rack lined with waxed paper.

Ethnic Breads

Bread is the most universal and the oldest food we have. The bread that dates back to Biblical days was very different from many of our rich sweet breads. It was the main diet of ancient peoples and was referred to as the "staff of life." Much of it was unleavened and was called flatbread. Chapatas and Peda are somewhat typical of these early breads. The United States has become the melting pot for many old recipes as well as for newer ideas that have evolved from many nationalities and regional or ethnic groups. In this section you'll find a variety of these old favorites, ones that have been handed down from generation to generation—all adapted for use with frozen doughs. The fun of serving these breads is not just that they are good; each one also has a little history.

All the baking information included at the beginning of the book and with each section applies to the recipes in this section. Many more ethnic breads can be found in the various sections of the book. Check the index for all the ethnic and nationality breads.

If frozen sweet bread dough is available in your supermarket, it can be used to make the ethnic coffee cakes. In recipes calling for raisins, you can substitute frozen raisin bread dough.

MORAVIAN COFFEE CAKE

The Pennsylvania Dutch coffee cake—a caramelized brown sugar mixture surrounds the bread loaf.

BAKE: 350° F. for 25 to 30 minutes   MAKES: 2 (9x5-inch) coffee cakes

1 loaf frozen white (or sweet) bread dough, thawed
½ cup brown sugar
1½ teaspoons cinnamon
¼ cup chopped nuts
6 tablespoons butter or margarine, melted

Let dough rise slightly. Divide in half; press each half into well-greased 9x5-inch pan. Combine brown sugar, cinnamon, and nuts; sprinkle over dough. Drizzle with butter. Cover; let rise in warm place until doubled in size, 1½ to 2 hours.

Bake at 350° F. for 25 to 30 minutes. Let stand a minute or two; carefully remove from pans.

STOLLEN

A holiday bread that had its origin in Germany. Years ago it was a breakfast bread, but today it is served with a cup of coffee any time of the day. It is shaped like an oversized Parker House roll and is full of Christmas fruits and almonds.

BAKE: 350° F. for 25 to 30 minutes   MAKES: 1 coffee cake

1 loaf frozen white (or sweet) bread dough, thawed
⅓ cup almond slices
¼ cup raisins
¼ cup mixed candied fruit
1 teaspoon grated orange peel
1 teaspoon grated lemon peel
butter or margarine
powdered sugar

Let dough rise slightly. Roll out on floured surface to a 14x9-inch rectangle. Sprinkle with almonds, fruit, and peels. Brush edge of dough with melted butter. Lift long side and fold over to within ½ inch of edge of other side. Place on greased cookie sheet. Cover; let rise in warm place until light or doubled in size, 1 to 1½ hours.

Bake at 350° F. for 25 to 30 minutes. Brush hot bread with soft or melted butter; sprinkle generously with powdered sugar.

GOLDEN BRAID

The Swiss, as well as bakers in other countries of Europe, demonstrate their baking skills by the number of strips of dough they can braid together. The beginner starts with three, and the expert can braid as many as nine strips together.

BAKE: 375° F. for 25 to 30 minutes   MAKES: 1 loaf

1 loaf frozen white (sweet or honey wheat) bread dough, thawed
1 tablespoon beaten egg
sesame seed

Let dough rise until almost doubled in size. Divide into thirds. Shape each into 15-inch strips. Braid together. Pinch ends together. Place on greased cookie sheet. Brush with egg, then sprinkle with sesame seed, if desired. Cover; let rise in warm place until very light, about 1 hour.

Bake at 375° F. for 25 to 30 minutes, or until a rich golden brown.

JUST FOR FUN: Divide dough into 4 pieces and braid together. Or, divide into 5 pieces and shape into 14-inch strips. Braid 3 together and place on cookie sheet. Twist 2 strips together, place on top of braid. Hold in place with wooden picks. Let rise and bake.

JULEKAKE

A fruit-filled bread found in almost all the Norwegian homes during the holiday season. Cardamom is one of the favorite spices of the Scandinavian countries.

BAKE: 350° F. for 25 to 30 minutes   MAKES: 2 round loaves

1 loaf frozen white (or sweet) bread dough, thawed
½ cup raisins
¼ cup cut candied cherries
¼ cup chopped almonds, if desired
½ teaspoon ground or crushed cardamom
   candied cherries
   almonds

Let dough rise until almost doubled in size. Flatten to ½-inch thickness. Sprinkle with the remaining ingredients; press down firmly. Divide in half; shape each into balls. Place in greased round cake pans or on a cookie sheet. Cover; let rise in warm place until light or doubled in size, 1 to 1½ hours.

Bake at 350° F. for 25 to 30 minutes. Frost warm loaves with Vanilla Icing, page 118. Decorate with candied cherries and almonds.

TRADITIONAL SHAPING: After shaping, make ½-inch horizontal cuts, about ½ inch from cookie sheet, all the way around the loaf. Press down in center of loaf with fist.

SALLY LUNN

This coffee cake was named after the girl who first made and sold it in her bakery in Bath, England. The delicate sugar-butter coating makes this adapted version taste much like the original.

BAKE: 375° F. for 30 to 35 minutes   MAKES: 1 bundt loaf

1 loaf frozen white (or sweet) bread dough, thawed
1½ tablespoons soft butter or margarine
3 tablespoons sugar

Butter a 9- or 12-cup bundt pan with 1 tablespoon butter. Sprinkle with 2 tablespoons sugar. Shape dough to 12-inch strip; seal ends together and place in pan. Brush with remaining butter; sprinkle with the remaining sugar. Cover; let rise in warm place until doubled in size, 1½ to 2 hours.

Bake at 375° F. for 30 to 35 minutes. (If bundt pan is heavy cast aluminum, decrease baking temperature to 350° F.)

POTICA
(Polish Holiday Bread)

Typical of Poland and Czechoslovakia are these little loaves of bread with a sweet filling swirled up on the inside. Honey is the popular sweetener.

BAKE: 350° F. for 30 to 35 minutes   MAKES: 2 small loaves

1 loaf frozen white (or sweet) bread dough, thawed

Let dough rise until almost doubled in size. Divide in half. Roll out one piece on floured surface to a 14x6-inch rectangle. Spread half of one of the fillings below to within ½ inch of sides. Moisten edges; roll up and seal seams. Place in greased 8x4- or 9x5-inch pan or on well-greased cookie sheet. Repeat with remaining dough. Cover; let rise in warm place until light, 30 minutes. (Do not let overrise.)

Bake at 350° F. for 30 to 35 minutes. Cool. To serve, cut into thin slices.

POPPY SEED FILLING:
Combine in small saucepan 1 cup finely chopped *nuts,* ⅓ cup *poppy seed,* ⅓ cup *cream,* ¼ cup *honey,* 2 tablespoons *sugar,* and 2 tablespoons *flour.* Cook over medium heat, stirring constantly, until thickened. Cool to warm.

WALNUT FILLING:
Combine in small saucepan 1½ cups finely chopped or ground *nuts,* ¼ cup *milk,* ⅓ cup *honey,* 2 tablespoons *flour,* and ½ teaspoon *cinnamon.* Cook over medium-low heat, stirring constantly, until thickened. Cool to warm.

COTTAGE CHEESE FILLING:
Combine 1 cup well-drained small curd *cottage cheese* (place in sieve and press down with spoon), ½ cup *raisins,* ¼ cup *sugar,* 1 small egg, 1 teaspoon grated *lemon peel,* and ½ teaspoon *cinnamon.*

DATE FILLING, PRUNE FILLING, APRICOT FILLING, OR APPLE FILLING:
Use Fillings for Swedish Tea Ring, page 96.

Ethnic Breads:
1. Swedish Tea Ring
2. Stollen
3. Kougelhof
4. Swiss Fried Bread
5. Kulich
6. Polish Babka
7. Julekake
8. Danish Kringle
9. Hot Cross Buns

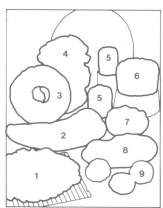

POLISH BABKA

A holiday bread from Poland—golden raisins, cinnamon, and lemon are unique to this bread. Bake it in a fancy mold or tube pan for a special touch.

BAKE: 350° F. for 30 to 35 minutes   MAKES: 1 round loaf

1 loaf frozen white (or sweet) bread dough, thawed
½ cup sultana (golden) raisins
1 teaspoon cinnamon
2 teaspoons grated lemon peel
Egg Wash, page 121, or milk
cinnamon and almond slices

Let dough rise until almost doubled in size. Flatten on floured surface to about ½ inch. Sprinkle with raisins, cinnamon, and peel. Roll up and knead some in order to distribute ingredients. Place in well-greased 1- or 1½-quart round casserole or mold. Cover; let rise in warm place until very light or more than doubled in size, about 1 hour.

Brush carefully with Egg Wash. Sprinkle with cinnamon and almonds. Bake at 350° F. for 30 to 35 minutes. Remove from pan immediately.

KULICH

Russian holiday bread. The breads are baked in tall cans. The rounded tops represent the domes of the old cathedrals of Russia. Lemon is one of the favorite flavors of Russia.

BAKE: 375° F. for 30 to 35 minutes   MAKES: 2 small tall loaves

1 loaf frozen white (or sweet) bread dough, thawed
½ cup raisins
¼ cup almond slices
2 teaspoons grated lemon peel

Let dough rise until almost doubled in size. Flatten to a 12x8-inch rectangle. Sprinkle with remaining ingredients. Roll up; cut in half. Shape each half into a ball. Press each ball into a well-greased 2-pound coffee can or 3-pound shortening can. Cover; let rise in warm place until doubled in size, 1 to 1½ hours. (Do not let rise too long.)

Bake at 375° F. for 30 to 35 minutes. Remove from cans immediately. Frost warm loaves with Vanilla Icing, page 118. Decorate with almonds and candied fruits.

OTHER CANS TO USE:
For 3 loaves, use 1-pound coffee cans or 30-ounce fruit cans. Baking time will be about 25 to 30 minutes.
For 4 loaves, use 1-pound shortening cans or 1-pound fruit and vegetable cans. Bake 20 to 25 minutes or until a golden brown.

GRECIAN FEAST BREAD

The ethnic bread traditionally served on religious days, especially Christmas and Easter. The 3 small loaves form a triangular shape which represents the Trinity. Each person is served a small slice from each loaf.

BAKE: 375° F. for 30 to 35 minutes   MAKES: 1 coffee bread

1 loaf frozen white (or sweet) bread dough, thawed
½ cup currants
Vanilla Icing, page 118
candied cherries
whole blanched almonds

Let dough rise slightly. Flatten to ½-inch thickness; sprinkle with currants. Fold in half, working currants into dough. Divide into thirds; shape each into a ball. Place ½ inch apart on greased cookie sheet, forming triangular shape. Cover; let rise in warm place until light or doubled in size, 1 to 1½ hours.

Bake at 375° F. for 30 to 35 minutes. Frost and make a flower on top of each loaf, using 3 almonds and 3 cherry pieces in each flower.

KOUGELHOF

A light, delicate coffee cake baked in a fluted tube pan and decorated with sugar-coated almonds. You'll like this Americanized version of the kougelhof.

BAKE: 375° F. for 30 to 35 minutes   MAKES: 1 bundt loaf

1 loaf frozen white (or sweet) bread dough, thawed
½ cup raisins
2 tablespoons soft butter or margarine
12 whole blanched almonds or 2 tablespoons almond slices
2 tablespoons sugar

Let dough rise until almost doubled in size. Spread butter in 9- or 12-cup bundt pan. Arrange almonds on bottom; sprinkle with sugar. Flatten dough to ½ inch; sprinkle with raisins. Roll up and shape into 12-inch strip. Seal ends together; place in prepared pan. Cover; let rise in warm place until light or doubled in size, 1 to 1½ hours.

Bake at 375° F. for 30 to 35 minutes. Remove from pan immediately. (If bundt pan is heavy cast aluminum, decrease baking temperature to 350° F.)

DANISH KRINGLE

*An easy way to make a flaky bread dough that looks almost like
the real Danish pastry.*

BAKE: 375° F. for 20 to 25 minutes   MAKES: 2 coffee cakes

1 loaf frozen white (or sweet) bread dough, thawed
¼ cup butter or margarine
1 cup sultana (golden) raisins
2 tablespoons butter or margarine
1 cup powdered sugar
2 to 3 teaspoons milk
½ teaspoon crushed or ground cardamom
1 tablespoon egg
1 tablespoon water
¼ cup sugar
¼ cup almond slices

Let dough rise until almost doubled in size. Roll out on floured surface
to a 14-inch square. Slice ¼ cup butter thinly over two-thirds of dough.
Fold unbuttered third over butter; then fold over the other third to make
three layers. Roll out again and fold in thirds. Place in plastic bag or
wrap in waxed paper; refrigerate at least 2 hours (or overnight).

Pour boiling water over raisins; let stand 1 hour and drain. Combine 2
tablespoons butter with powdered sugar and cardamom. Add milk just
until mixture is of spreading consistency.

Roll out dough on floured surface to an 18x12-inch rectangle. Spread
with frosting. Sprinkle with raisins. Cut in half to make two 18x6-inch
strips. Roll up each strip, starting with 18-inch side. Stretch to 24 inches
and place, seam-side up, on greased cookie sheets in pretzel shape.
Flatten to about ¼ inch. Combine egg and water; brush over tops.
Combine sugar and almonds. Sprinkle over coffee cakes. Cover; let rise
in warm place 30 minutes.

Bake at 375° F. for 20 to 25 minutes, or until rich golden brown.

DANISH PASTRIES:
Prepare dough as directed in first paragraph for Danish Kringle. Roll out
chilled dough to 16-inch square. Cut into 4-inch squares. Top each with a
spoonful of *almond paste, jam,* or sweetened *applesauce.* Moisten edges; fold
in half and seal. Brush tops with egg mixture and sprinkle with sugar and
almonds. Place on greased cookie sheets. Cover, let rise, and bake 15 to 20
minutes.

HOUSKA

The braided Bohemian Holiday bread—Houska generally has 9 strips, with a 4-strip braid on the bottom, a 3-strip braid in the middle, and 2 strips braided together on top. This recipe is a simplified version, using a braid of 3 on the bottom, and 2 strips twisted together on top.

BAKE: 350° F. for 30 to 35 minutes   MAKES: 1 loaf

1 loaf frozen white (or sweet) bread dough, thawed
¼ cup mixed candied fruit
½ cup raisins
¼ cup almond slices
2 tablespoons sugar
1 tablespoon egg
1 teaspoon water
whole blanched almonds

Let dough rise until doubled in size. Roll out on floured surface to a 14-inch square. Sprinkle with fruits, almonds, and sugar; press firmly into dough. Cut into 5 strips. Roll up each lengthwise, sealing seam. Braid 3 strips together; place on well-greased cookie sheet. Twist the 2 strips together; place on braid. Insert several wooden picks to hold together. Combine egg and water; brush over braid. Insert whole blanched almonds here and there in braid. Cover; let rise in warm place until light or doubled in size, 30 to 60 minutes.

Bake at 350° F. for 30 to 35 minutes.

AMERICAN CHAPATIES

Adapted from the Indian unleavened flatbread. Fun to serve with a curry dinner.

FRY: 4 to 5 minutes on a hot griddle   MAKES: 16

1 loaf honey wheat or white bread dough, thawed
butter

Let dough rise until doubled in size. Divide into 16 pieces. Roll out and stretch to make a 6-inch paper-thin circle, turning over and re-flouring surface as needed. Immediately fry on medium-hot heavily buttered griddle 4 to 5 minutes, turning to brown both sides. Add butter as each piece is fried. Best hot from the griddle. Or make the breads early, place them on cookie sheet, and reheat in oven a few minutes.

IDEAS: Chapaties are good plain or as a snack with a zesty dip. They make a good Sunday lunch topped with honey or maple syrup and served with sausage or bacon. Or substitute them for taco shells or a tortilla for a Mexican treat.

ITALIAN EASTER EGG BREAD

Traditional to most of the countries of Southern Europe or along the Mediterranean Sea is this braided ring with colored eggs baked right into the loaf.

BAKE: 375° F. for 20 to 25 minutes   MAKES: 1 large ring

1 loaf frozen white (or sweet) bread dough, thawed
6 or 8 plain or colored uncooked eggs*
1 tablespoon egg or egg white
2 teaspoons water

Let dough rise until doubled in size. Divide in half. Shape each half into a 24-inch strip. Twist the two strips together. Place on greased cookie sheet in a ring, sealing ends together. Combine egg and water; brush over bread. Insert uncooked eggs into the twisted loaf. Cover; let rise in warm place until light or doubled in size, 30 to 60 minutes.

Bake at 375° F. for 20 to 25 minutes. Frost warm ring with Vanilla Icing, page 118. (Do not frost eggs.) Sprinkle with multicolored decorettes, if desired.

*Color eggs as recommended on Easter egg coloring kit.

HOT CROSS BUNS

This English bun was first made to honor the goddess of spring. With the coming of the Christian faith, the addition of the cross has made it symbolic of Good Friday.

BAKE: 400° F. for 12 to 15 minutes   MAKES: 12 to 16 rolls

1 loaf frozen white (or sweet) bread dough, thawed
½ cup currants
½ teaspoon cinnamon
2 tablespoons chopped candied citron, if desired

Let dough rise slightly. Flatten dough to ¼- to ½-inch thickness. Sprinkle with fruits and cinnamon; press down firmly. Roll up; cut into 12 to 16 pieces. Shape into balls, making sure currants are covered. Place 2 inches apart on greased cookie sheet. Cover; let rise in warm place until light or doubled in size, 1 to 1½ hours.

Bake at 400° F. for 12 to 15 minutes. Make a cross on each bun with frosting. Use half the recipe for Vanilla Icing, page 118.

SWISS FRIED BREAD

Crisp fried breads that substitute for dessert or cookies. Fun for an after-the-game snack, a tailgating party, or a family treat on a cold winter night.

DEEP FAT FRY: 350° F. for 1 to 2 minutes   MAKES: 16

1 loaf frozen white bread dough, thawed
powdered or granulated sugar

Let dough rise until doubled in size. Divide into 16 pieces. Roll out each piece until very thin on floured surface to about a 6-inch circle. Re-flour surface while rolling if necessary. Fry immediately in deep hot fat (350° F.) for 1 to 2 minutes, turning every 15 seconds until golden brown on both sides. (Metal tongs work best for turning.) Drain on absorbent paper. To serve, sprinkle with sugar.

NOTE: Fry one at a time.

PEDA

A flatbread popular in the Eastern Mediterranean countries.

BAKE: 450° F. for 10 to 15 minutes   MAKES: 6 (9-inch) flatbreads

1 loaf frozen white (or honey wheat) bread dough, thawed
3 tablespoons butter or margarine, melted

Let dough rise until doubled in size. Divide into sixths. Roll out and stretch each piece on floured surface to a 9-inch circle. Place on greased cookie sheets. Brush generously with butter. Bake *immediately* at 450° F. for 10 to 15 minutes. (Flatbread puffs in spots while baking and does not brown evenly.) Serve hot as a snack or dinner bread.

For thin, crisp and crackery flatbreads, divide into 9 pieces. Roll out and stretch paper-thin to 9-inch circles. Bake at 425° F. for 5 to 8 minutes; watch closely.

TAOS INDIAN BREAD

This loaf is shaped the way the Pueblo Indians shaped their bread to honor the sun god.

BAKE: 375° F. for 25 to 30 minutes   MAKES: 2 loaves

1 loaf frozen white bread dough, thawed

Let dough rise until almost doubled in size. Roll out half of dough to a 10-inch circle. Fold in half; place on greased cookie sheet. Make 6 cuts, 2 inches deep, from outside toward fold. Bring folded ends together to make a circle for "sun" and "rays." Cover; let rise in warm place until light or doubled in size, about 1 hour.

Bake at 375° F. for 25 to 30 minutes. Brush hot loaves with butter.

SWEDISH TEA RING

This festive coffee cake from Sweden is popular any time of the year. In Sweden it is called a Klippta Kransor, meaning "a cut dough". To us the most common filling is cinnamon and sugar, but any of the fillings below can be used.

BAKE: 375° F. for 20 to 25 minutes   MAKES: 1 round coffee cake

1 loaf frozen white (or sweet) bread dough, thawed
1 tablespoon butter or margarine, soft or melted

Let dough rise until doubled in size. Prepare one of the fillings below. Roll out dough on floured surface to a 15x12-inch rectangle. Brush with butter; sprinkle or spread with filling. Roll up, starting with 15-inch side. Form into a ring on well-greased cookie sheet; seal ends together. Make cuts ¾ inch apart, almost to center of ring. Turn cuts on sides. Cover; let rise in warm place until light or doubled in size, 30 to 60 minutes.

Bake at 375° F. for 20 to 25 minutes. Frost warm ring with Vanilla Icing, page 118.

NOTE: For easier pan washing, line cookie sheet with foil; then grease.

TEA RING FILLINGS:

CINNAMON-SUGAR FILLING: Combine ⅓ cup *sugar*, ¼ cup chopped *nuts, raisins,* or *coconut,* and 1 teaspoon *cinnamon.*

PRUNE OR APRICOT FILLING: Cook 1 cup cut dried *prunes* or *apricots* and 3 tablespoons *sugar* in ⅓ cup *orange juice* or water until thick and tender. Stir in ¼ cup chopped *nuts,* if desired.

APPLE FILLING: Shred 2 pared *apples.* Combine with ¼ cup *sugar,* ¼ cup *raisins,* and ½ teaspoon *cinnamon.*

MINCEMEAT FILLING: Use 1 cup prepared *mincemeat.*

POPPY SEED FILLING: Combine in small saucepan ¾ cup finely chopped *walnuts,* ¼ cup *poppy seed,* 2 tablespoons each *honey,* melted *butter, milk,* and *flour.* Cook until thick.

CHRISTMAS FILLING: Combine ¼ cup *sugar,* ½ teaspoon *cardamom,* ¼ cup *almond slices,* and ½ cup mixed *candied fruit.*

COTTAGE CHEESE FILLING: Combine 1 cup well-drained creamed *cottage cheese,* ¼ cup *sugar,* 1 teaspoon grated *orange peel,* and ¼ cup *raisins.* Sprinkle with *cinnamon* after spreading filling on dough.

DATE FILLING: Cook 1 cup *dates,* 2 tablespoons *sugar,* 1 tablespoon *lemon juice,* and ¼ cup *water* until thick.

ORANGE-COCONUT FILLING: Combine ¼ cup *sugar,* ½ cup *coconut,* and 2 tablespoons grated *orange peel.*

Supper and Snack Breads

Any time we can combine our meat and bread into one dish we are saving time. Many of the ideas in this chapter are not only fun to serve but also economical. They make good Saturday night or Sunday supper ideas.

To go along with our casual way of living are a number of snack breads. They are a refreshing change for an appetizer and probably lower in calories than some of the snacks you have been serving. Many of the snack breads include good protein and make a good light supper or buffet idea or after-school snack.

Whenever a baked bread contains a perishable item, be sure to refrigerate the leftovers.

DEEP DISH PIZZA

Another type of pizza, popular in Italy, is the Sicilian pizza.
It has a thicker crust and filling.

BAKE: 425° F. for 15 to 20 minutes   MAKES: 3 (9-inch) pizzas

1 loaf frozen white bread dough, thawed
1 to 1½ pounds ground beef or unseasoned pork sausage
1 small onion, chopped
1 can (4 oz.) mushroom stems and pieces, undrained
1 cup (8 oz.) canned or cooked tomatoes
1 can (6 oz.) tomato paste
½ teaspoon each: salt, sugar, oregano, basil, marjoram
½ teaspoon garlic powder
2 tablespoons chopped fresh parsley
1 cup shredded Mozzarella or pizza cheese

Let dough rise until doubled in size. Cook meat and onion in skillet until meat loses red color. Drain off fat. Stir in remaining ingredients except cheese. Cover; simmer 15 minutes. Cool to warm.

Divide dough into thirds. Press each piece into bottom and sides of well-greased 9-inch pie pan. Spoon filling into shells; spread to cover bottom. Sprinkle with cheese. Let stand 15 minutes.

Bake at 425° F. for 15 to 20 minutes, or until crust is rich golden brown. Serve hot.

TUNA FLIP

A giant Parker House roll is filled with tuna and cheese.

BAKE: 375° F. for 25 to 30 minutes   MAKES: 4 servings and 8 dinner rolls

½ loaf frozen white bread dough, thawed*
1 can (6 ½ oz.) tuna, drained
½ cup shredded Cheddar cheese or pizza cheese
½ cup chopped celery
2 tablespoons chopped onion
2 tablespoons chopped green pepper
½ teaspoon dill seed, if desired
⅛ teaspoon pepper

Let dough rise until doubled in size. Combine tuna with remaining ingredients. Roll out half the dough on floured surface to a 12x10-inch rectangle. Place tuna along a 12-inch side. Fold uncovered dough over tuna; moisten edges and seal. With sharp knife, make several slits on the top. Place on greased cookie sheet. Cover; let rise in warm place 30 minutes.

Bake at 375° F. for 25 to 30 minutes. Serve warm. If desired, top with a cheese sauce.

*Use the other half of the loaf to make dinner rolls or to make a second Tuna Flip. Baked loaf may be frozen and used at a later time.

VARIATIONS:

GROUND BEEF FILLING: Brown together 1 pound *ground beef* and ¼ cup chopped *onion*. Stir in ½ teaspoon *salt*, ⅛ teaspoon *pepper*, and 2 tablespoons *catsup*. If desired, top meat mixture with cheese slices.

CHICKEN FILLING: Combine 1 cup cooked cubed *chicken* or *turkey*, ½ cup canned or fresh *mushrooms*, ½ teaspoon *salt*, and a pinch each: *thyme, basil, parsley, pepper,* and *oregano*. Top with *Swiss cheese* slices.

Supper and Snack Breads:
1. Chip Dip
2. Bite-Sized Stuffies
3. Miniature Bow Knots
4. Snack Sticks
5. Tuna Flip
6. Pigs-in-Blankets
7. Super Sandwiches
8. Cheese Bubble Loaf
9. Beef Bake
10. Cheese Bacon Snack Bread
11. Onion Toppers
12. Hamburger-Stuffed Rolls

LUNCHEON BUBBLE RING

Herb-coated bubbles form a ring that can be filled with salad or a hot entrée for an easy supper or a festive luncheon.

BAKE: 350° F. for 25 to 30 minutes   MAKES: 6 to 8 servings

12 frozen dough dinner rolls
2 tablespoons butter or margarine, melted
¼ teaspoon each: garlic powder, thyme, oregano, parsley, marjoram

Combine butter and herbs. Coat each roll with butter mixture. Place in 6½-cup ring mold. Cover; let rise until very light or doubled in size. (See package label for rising time of frozen rolls.)

Bake at 350° F. for 25 to 30 minutes. Remove from pan immediately. Fill center with a tuna, turkey, or shrimp salad or a hot entrée such as Western Barbecue Beef.

WESTERN BARBECUE BEEF:
Brown together 1 pound *ground beef* and ½ cup chopped *onion*. Stir in ¾ cup *catsup*, 2 tablespoons *brown sugar*, 2 tablespoons *lemon juice*, 1 teaspoon *salt*, 1 teaspoon *Worcestershire sauce*, ½ teaspoon *dry mustard*, ¼ teaspoon *pepper*, and ¼ cup *water*. Cover; simmer 30 minutes. Spoon into center of ring and garnish with shredded *cheese* and *parsley*, if desired.

SHRIMP SALAD:
Toss together in a large mixing bowl: 2 cups cooked tiny *shrimp* or larger shrimp cut into pieces, 1 cup green *grapes*, halved, 1 cup head *lettuce* chunks, 1 cup thinly sliced *celery*, 2 hard-cooked *eggs*, chopped, ½ cup *salad dressing* or mayonnaise, ½ teaspoon *curry powder*, *salt*, and white *pepper* to taste. Garnish salad with *tomato* wedges or slices of hard-cooked *egg*.

NOTE: White pepper is often suggested for sauces and salads because it does not leave tiny black specks.

PIGS-IN-BLANKETS

A fun supper idea that's sure to please the youngsters—hot dogs wrapped in a blanket of bread.

BAKE: 375° F. for 15 to 20 minutes   MAKES: 16 (8 servings)

1 loaf frozen white (honey wheat or French) bread dough, thawed
16 frankfurters or pre-cooked sausages
mustard, pickle relish, or catsup, if desired

Let dough rise until doubled in size. Divide into 16 pieces. Flatten each to a 4-inch square on floured surface. Place a little mustard or other seasoning sauce in center. Top with frankfurter; bring dough around and seal well. Place, seam-side down, on greased cookie sheet. Cover; let rise in warm place 30 minutes.

Bake at 375° F. for 15 to 20 minutes. Serve warm.

SUPER SANDWICHES

A good way to use small amounts of leftover meats. Make all the sandwiches the same or make an assortment.

BAKE: 400° F. for 12 to 15 minutes   MAKES: 12 sandwiches

1 loaf frozen (any flavor) bread dough, thawed
soft butter
meats and cheeses (see below)
mustard, barbecue sauce, catsup, as desired

Let dough rise until doubled in size. Divide into 12 pieces. Flatten to 5-inch circle. Dot center with a small amount of butter. Place a generous amount of 3x2-inch pieces of meat and/or cheese on each. Dot with mustard or a seasoning sauce. Moisten edges; fold in half and seal well. Prick top with fork. Cover; let rise in warm place 30 minutes.

Bake at 400° F. for 12 to 15 minutes. Serve warm or cold. Do not keep unrefrigerated for a long period of time.

MEATS AND CHEESES:

HAM SANDWICHES: Slices or cubes of baked or boiled *ham* and *mustard* or well-drained *pickle relish*.

HAM AND CHEESE SANDWICHES: *Ham* as above and Swiss or pizza *cheese*. Cheddar cheese can be used too, but be sure to seal well.

CORNED BEEF SANDWICHES: Use slices or cubes of *corned beef* with Swiss or other *cheese* and a small spoonful of well-drained *sauerkraut*. Season with one or more of the following: *mustard, horseradish sauce, caraway seed* or *mayonnaise*.

ROAST BEEF OR PORK SANDWICHES: Slices or pieces of roasted *beef* or *pork* (good use for leftover pieces) seasoned with *barbecue sauce* or with *mushrooms* and a small spoonful of thickened *gravy*.

SALAMI SANDWICHES: Use any kind of cold cut *meats* cut in small pieces and stacked; season as desired. Add slices of *cheese* or *pickles*, if desired.

CHOPPED BEEF SANDWICHES: Thin-sliced chopped pressed *beef, ham, corned beef* or *turkey* makes good sandwiches. Use it alone or in combination with *cheese* and other seasonings.

TURKEY OR CHICKEN SANDWICHES: Slices of cooked *turkey*, seasoned with *salt* and *pepper*, plain or in combination with Swiss or pizza *cheese*.

TUNA-CHEESE SANDWICHES: Use *tuna* alone or in combination with a *cheese*.

(These are just a few filling combinations that can go into Super Sandwiches. Sandwiches can be baked and frozen and then be ready to take on a picnic or a boating, camping, or fishing trip. The sandwiches can be served warm or cold.)

BEEF PASTIES

Adapted from the pasty that was lunch for miners in Cornwall, England. These same pasties have been a popular food in the iron-mining areas of Minnesota and the Upper Peninsula of Michigan. The original was baked inside a pastry crust. The bread covering makes these pasties taste much like a beef sandwich.

BAKE: 375° F. for 15 to 20 minutes   MAKES: 6 large pasties

1 loaf frozen white bread dough, thawed
1 pound lean ground beef (1 ½ pounds regular)
1 medium potato, pared and chopped
1 carrot, pared and chopped
1 medium onion, chopped
1 stalk celery, chopped
1 teaspoon salt
⅛ teaspoon pepper
1 teaspoon mixed herbs (thyme, oregano, marjoram, parsley)

Let dough rise until doubled in size. Combine remaining ingredients in large skillet; cook 20 minutes. Cool to lukewarm. Divide dough into 6 pieces; roll out and stretch each on floured surface to 8-inch circle. Top each with about ⅔ cup filling. Moisten edges; fold in half and seal well. With scissors, snip a short gash on top of each. Place on greased cookie sheet. Cover; let rise in warm place 30 minutes.

Bake at 375° F. for 15 to 20 minutes. Serve warm. (Can be served cold, but keep refrigerated until serving time.)

TURKEY PASTIES:
Combine in skillet 1 pound *ground turkey*, 2 tablespoons *butter* or margarine, 1 medium *potato*, pared and chopped, 1 *carrot*, pared and chopped, 1 medium *onion*, chopped, 1 stalk *celery*, chopped, 1 teaspoon *salt*, 1 teaspoon *parsley*, ½ teaspoon *sage*, ¼ teaspoon *thyme*, and ⅛ teaspoon *pepper*. Cook 20 minutes. Cool to lukewarm. Substitute for beef filling in recipe above.

NOTE: For medium-sized pasties, divide dough into 12 pieces and roll each to 6-inch circle and top with ⅓ cup filling.

BEEF BAKE

Butter crumb bubbles bake on top of a gourmet beef casserole.

BAKE: 375° F. for 25 to 30 minutes   MAKES: 6 to 8 servings

½ loaf frozen white bread dough, thawed*
1 to 2 pounds round steak, cut in thin strips
2 tablespoons butter or other shortening
1 cup sliced onion
2 tablespoons flour
2 cups canned or fresh sliced tomatoes
1 tablespoon sugar
1 teaspoon each salt, minced parsley
¼ teaspoon each marjoram, basil, thyme
½ to 1 cup fresh or canned mushrooms
1 cup dairy sour cream
3 tablespoons butter or margarine, melted
⅓ cup bread crumbs

Brown steak in butter in 10-inch skillet; add onions and sauté a few minutes. Stir in flour, then tomatoes and seasonings. Cover; simmer 1½ to 2 hours or until meat is tender. Remove from heat; add mushrooms and cream.

Divide a half-loaf of bread into 10 pieces. Dip pieces in butter; then coat with bread crumbs. Place on top of warm mixture. Cover; let rise until dough is light or doubled in size, about 1 hour.

Uncover and bake at 375° F. for 25 to 30 minutes.

*Shape the other half of the loaf into dinner rolls; let rise and bake. Before baking, the rolls may be dipped in butter and rolled in crumbs, if desired.

ONION KUCHEN

A creamy onion mixture tops dinner bread. A good bread with a roast beef or pork dinner.

BAKE: 375° F. for 25 to 30 minutes   MAKES: 13x9-inch bread

1 loaf frozen white bread dough, thawed
1½ cups chopped onion
2 tablespoons butter or margarine
1 cup small curd cottage cheese, drained
1 egg
2 teaspoons caraway seed, if desired

Let dough rise slightly. Sauté onion in butter. Stir in remaining ingredients. Press dough into well-greased 13x9-inch pan. Top with onion mixture. Cover; let rise in warm place until doubled in size, 30 to 60 minutes.

Bake at 375° F. for 25 to 30 minutes. Best warm or the first day. Leftover bread should be refrigerated.

SKILLET BEEF-BURGER

The family will like this—a sloppy Joe mixture cooked under light and tender rolls.

BAKE: 375° F. for 25 to 30 minutes   MAKES: 6 servings

½ loaf frozen white bread dough, thawed*
1 ½ pounds ground beef
¼ cup chopped onions
1 can (4 oz.) mushroom stems and pieces, undrained
1 cup (8 oz.) tomato sauce or canned tomatoes
2 tablespoons catsup
¼ teaspoon each oregano, thyme, marjoram, parsley
½ teaspoon salt
⅛ teaspoon pepper

Brown beef and onions in 10-inch skillet. Add remaining ingredients except bread dough. Cover; simmer 15 minutes. Cool to warm.
Divide half of loaf of dough into 20 pieces and place on top of warm beef mixture. Cover; let rise 30 minutes or until pieces of bread dough have doubled in size.

Bake uncovered at 375° F. for 25 to 30 minutes. Serve from skillet.

*Make dinner rolls or 3 small mini-loaves from the other half of the dough.

SKILLET TURKEY-BURGER:
Substitute 1 pound *ground turkey* for the ground beef. Brown the turkey and onions in 2 tablespoons *butter* or margarine.

ONION TOPPERS

Onion in cream cheese bakes on top of rolls. A beautiful touch to an easy buffet supper.

BAKE: 375° F. for 15 to 20 minutes   MAKES: 16 rolls

1 loaf frozen white bread dough, thawed
1 ½ cups chopped onion
2 tablespoons butter or margarine
⅓ cup (3 oz.) cream cheese
¼ teaspoon salt
1 teaspoon crushed dill seed, if desired

Let dough rise until almost doubled in size. Sauté onion in butter. Stir in cream cheese, salt, and dill. Divide dough into 16 pieces. Shape each into 3-inch flat round. Place 2 inches apart on greased cookie sheets. Cover; let rise in warm place until light or doubled in size, about 1 hour.

Press deep hole in center of each with floured fingers. Fill with tablespoonful onion mixture. Bake at 375° F. for 15 to 20 minutes. Best warm the day they are baked.

HAMBURGER-STUFFED ROLLS

The whole family will love these stuffed rolls—just a little bit of bread surrounds the patty.

BAKE: 400° F. for 15 to 20 minutes   MAKES: 16 (8 servings)

1 loaf frozen white bread dough, thawed
2 pounds ground beef
½ cup finely chopped onion
1½ teaspoons salt
¼ teaspoon pepper
½ teaspoon chili powder
1 teaspoon soy sauce

Let dough rise until doubled in size. Meanwhile prepare hamburgers: Combine ground beef with remaining ingredients and shape into 16 balls. Fry in large skillet 10 minutes, turning once. Cool to warm on absorbent paper.

Divide dough into 16 pieces. Flatten and shape around meat; seal seams together well. Place, seam-side down, on greased cookie sheet. Cover; let rise in warm place 30 minutes.

Bake at 400° F. for 15 to 20 minutes. Serve warm or cold with catsup or chili sauce. (If served as a cold sandwich, keep refrigerated until serving time.)

TURKEY-STUFFED ROLLS:
Combine 1½ pounds *ground turkey*, ¼ cup finely chopped *onion*, ¼ cup finely chopped *celery*, 1½ teaspoons *salt*, ½ teaspoon *sage*, ½ teaspoon *thyme*, ½ teaspoon *parsley*, ¼ teaspoon *pepper*, and ¼ cup *cream*. Shape into 16 balls. Fry 10 minutes. Cool to warm. Shape bread dough around balls; let rise and bake as directed for hamburgers.

HAM-STUFFED ROLLS:
Combine 1½ pounds *ground ham*, 1 cup dry *bread crumbs*, 1 egg, and ½ cup shredded Cheddar or American *cheese*. Shape into 16 balls. Do not fry. Shape bread dough around balls; let rise and bake as directed.

BITE-SIZED STUFFIES

For a crunchy crust, dip shaped rolls in melted butter, then Parmesan cheese.

BAKE: 400° F. for 10 to 12 minutes   MAKES: 36 buns

1 loaf frozen white bread dough, thawed
36 cubes of ham, luncheon meats, cheese, or shrimp

Let dough rise slightly. Divide into thirds; then divide each third into 12 pieces. Shape each piece around meat or cheese; seal well. Place on greased cookie sheet. Cover; let rise in warm place until light or doubled in size, 30 to 60 minutes.

Bake at 400° F. for 10 to 12 minutes. Brush hot rolls with plain or garlic butter.

PIZZA

Season pizza to suit your family's taste. If you want, use an already prepared mix for the sauce and add your favorite topping. If you don't need both pizzas, one can be frozen and reheated at another time.

BAKE: 450° F. for 15 to 20 minutes   MAKES 2 (13-inch) pizzas

1 loaf frozen white bread dough, thawed
½ cup finely chopped onion
1 tablespoon olive or cooking oil
1 cup (8 oz.) tomato sauce
¾ cup (6 oz.) tomato paste
1 clove garlic, mashed and chopped
½ teaspoon salt
1 teaspoon sugar
½ teaspoon oregano
¼ teaspoon basil
pinch of pepper
2 cups shredded Mozzarella or pizza cheese
fresh parsley
Parmesan cheese

Let dough rise until doubled in size. Sauté onion in oil. Add next 8 ingredients. Simmer 5 minutes. Roll out half of dough on floured surface to a 13-inch circle. Place in greased pizza pan or on greased cookie sheet. Brush with oil; sprinkle with ½ cup cheese and top with half the tomato mixture. If desired, sprinkle with a topping, then ½ cup cheese, parsley, and Parmesan cheese. Repeat with remaining dough.

Bake immediately at 450° F. for 15 to 20 minutes. Serve hot.

PIZZA TOPPINGS:
Quantities given are for one pizza. You may double the amount for both pizzas, or use a different topping on each pizza.
  ½ cup cooked pork *sausage*
  ½ cup fresh or canned sliced *mushrooms*
  6 or 7 *anchovies*
  ½ cup diced, sliced or strips of *pepperoni, salami,* or other Italian *sausages*
  ½ cup tiny or chopped *shrimp*
  ½ cup cooked *ground beef*
  ½ cup sliced *frankfurters* or bologna
  ¼ cup crumbled fried *bacon*
  ½ cup chopped ripe *olives*
  ½ cup *tuna*

PIZZA PARTY: *Let dough thaw and rise. Divide into 6 parts. Press each into bottom of greased 9-inch pie pan. Sprinkle with cheese and spread with tomato sauce, a topping, and more cheese. Bake at 450° F. for 15 to 20 minutes. If desired, pizzas may be made and then frozen. Bake frozen pizzas. (It's always fun to have sauces and toppings ready and then let each person put a pizza together.)*

CHEESE SNACK BREAD

A thin layer of bread under a peppy topping makes a good patio or tailgate party snack.

BAKE: 375° F. for 20 to 25 minutes   MAKES: 15x10-inch bread

1 loaf frozen white bread dough, thawed
2 tablespoons butter or margarine, melted
½ teaspoon onion or garlic salt
½ teaspoon smoke sauce, if desired
2 cups shredded Cheddar or American cheese

Let dough rise until almost doubled in size. Press into or roll out to fit greased 15x10-inch pan or onto cookie sheet. Combine butter and seasonings; brush over dough. Sprinkle with cheese. Cover; let rise in warm place until light, 30 minutes.

Bake at 375° F. for 20 to 25 minutes, or until bread is golden brown. Best warm. Cut into sticks.

CHEESE BACON SNACK BREAD:
Sprinkle 1 cup shredded Cheddar or American cheese and ¼ pound crumbled fried bacon over top.

ONION SNACK BREAD:
Sauté 2 cups chopped onion in 2 tablespoons butter. Combine with 1 beaten egg and ¼ cup cream or evaporated milk, and 1 teaspoon celery seed. Spoon over dough. Sprinkle with shredded cheese, if desired.

FRENCH SNACK BREAD:
Combine ¼ pound crumbled fried bacon, 1 cup shredded Swiss or pizza cheese, ¼ teaspoon salt, ⅛ teaspoon white pepper, 1 beaten egg, and ½ cup light cream or undiluted evaporated milk. Spoon over dough.

STUFFED PARMESAN ROLLS

These rolls have a pocket of cheese on the inside and are coated with cheese on the outside.

BAKE: 375° F. for 15 to 18 minutes   MAKES: 16 rolls

1 loaf frozen white (or honey wheat) bread dough, thawed
16 (¾-inch) Cheddar cheese cubes
melted butter
Parmesan cheese

Let dough rise slightly. Divide into 16 pieces. Shape into balls around cheese cubes. Dip tops into butter, then Parmesan cheese. Place 3 inches apart, cheese-side up, on greased cookie sheet. Cover; let rise in warm place until very light or doubled in size, 1 to 1½ hours.

Bake at 375° F. for 15 to 18 minutes.

PARMESAN DINNER ROLLS:
Omit the cheese cubes in the above rolls.

TUNA COCKTAIL TWIRLS

Tuna and cream cheese are rolled up in tiny appetizer rolls.
Or use these rolls for a salad luncheon.

BAKE: 375° F. for 15 to 20 minutes   MAKES: 36 small rolls

1 loaf frozen white (or honey wheat) bread dough, thawed
1 can (6½ oz.) tuna
1 package (8 oz.) cream cheese, room temperature
2 tablespoons cream or milk
½ cup chopped pimento-stuffed olives, if desired
½ teaspoon curry powder

Let dough rise until doubled in size. Soften cheese with cream; combine with remaining ingredients. Roll out dough on floured surface to a 16x10-inch rectangle. Spread with filling; cut in half to make two 16x5-inch rectangles. Roll up each, starting with 16-inch side. Cut each into 18 pieces. Place, cut-side down, on greased cookie sheets. Cover; let rise in warm place until light or doubled in size, 30 to 60 minutes.

Bake at 375° F. for 15 to 20 minutes. Best warm. When cool, keep refrigerated, and then warm just before serving.

NOTE: Other ground cooked meat fillings can be substituted for the tuna. Use the meat with the cream cheese or as is.

CHEESE BUBBLE LOAF

A dinner loaf made up of tiny bubbles that are filled with cubes of cheese. Serve it warm, and each person can pull off a bubble. Or slice it when cold and each piece will have a patchwork of cheese. For other fillings, see note below.

BAKE: 375° F. for 30 to 35 minutes   MAKES: 1 loaf

1 loaf frozen white (or honey wheat) bread dough, thawed
36 (½-inch) cubes Cheddar or American cheese

Divide dough into thirds; then divide each third into 12 pieces. Shape each piece around a cube of cheese. Layer balls in a well-greased 9x5-inch pan. Cover; let rise in warm place until dough well fills the pan, 1½ to 2 hours.

Bake at 375° F. for 30 to 35 minutes. Refrigerate leftover bread.

SUGGESTION: Try one of the following for the cheese—cubes of ham, canned luncheon meats, summer sausage, baked meatloaf, or tiny cooked meatballs.

MINIATURE DINNER ROLLS

Tiny rolls to fill with salad filling or tiny squares of meat and cheese—fine for receptions and open houses.

BAKE: 400° F. for 10 to 12 minutes   MAKES: 36 small rolls

1 loaf frozen white (or honey wheat) bread dough, thawed

Let dough rise slightly. Divide into thirds; then divide each third into 12 pieces. Shape into balls; place on greased cookie sheet. Cover; let rise in warm place until light or doubled in size, 45 to 60 minutes.

Bake at 400° F. for 10 to 12 minutes.

MINIATURE BOW KNOTS:
Shape tiny pieces of dough into 4-inch strips. Tie into knots. Let rise and bake as directed above.

SNACK STICKS:
Divide dough into fourths, then into 12 pieces. Shape each piece into 4-inch stick. Brush hot baked sticks with Garlic Butter, page 120. Serve with a chip dip. Makes 48.

CHIP DIP:
Combine 1 cup dairy *sour cream,* 1 package dry *onion soup mix,* and 1 teaspoon *dill seed.*

COCKTAIL MEATBALLS

Split the miniature dinner rolls, above, and fill with the meatballs—good for a snack or as part of a buffet supper.

SIMMER: 45 minutes   MAKES: 36 small meatballs

1 ½ pounds ground beef
⅓ cup finely chopped onion
¼ cup bread crumbs
2 tablespoons milk
1 teaspoon salt
⅛ teaspoon pepper

Combine all ingredients; mix thoroughly. Shape into 1-inch balls; then flatten to ½ inch. (Keep hands moist for easy shaping.) Brown in hot greased skillet. Drain off fat. Pour Barbecue Sauce over meatballs. Cover and simmer or bake in 350° F. oven 45 minutes.

BARBECUE SAUCE: Combine ¼ cup chopped *onion,* 1 cup *catsup,* 1 tablespoon *brown sugar,* 1 tablespoon *lemon juice,* 1 teaspoon *salt,* 1 teaspoon *Worcestershire sauce,* a pinch of *pepper,* a pinch of *cloves,* and a drop of *smoke sauce.* Pour over meatballs. (This sauce is also good with leftover beef or pork roast for a barbecued beef sandwich. Simmer sauce 30 minutes; then add meat and reheat.)

Breads Men Like to Bake

Many of our best chefs and bakers are men, but baking and cooking are no longer just for the man who is a professional. More and more men are baking and cooking or experimenting with foods just for the satisfaction that comes with it. Most men prefer to experiment with special dishes rather than routine cooking. That's where bread baking comes into the picture. You can do it just for fun, or it can be therapeutic —if tensions are running high, take them out on a loaf of bread dough. Or add your touch to a dinner entrée or appetizer by complementing it with a special, special bread.

The best proof of success is a beautiful loaf of homebaked bread. It's a lot easier and takes much less time when you start with frozen bread dough. A good idea is to place the frozen dough in the refrigerator the night before. Then it's all ready to go when you come home from work.

On the next few pages are bread recipes with a masculine flair. You'll find many more throughout the book; this section is just a teaser. Remember—herbs, spices and other seasonings can be varied to suit your taste. It is generally not a good idea to vary filling quantities because they have been developed to the best amount for a loaf of dough. After baking a number of recipes from this book, you are going to discover some of your own ideas.

Other recipes in this book that you will want to try are: Butter Crust Vienna Bread, Skillet Beef-Burger, Bacon-Cheese Swirl, Skillet Bread, Down-to-Earth Bread, Crazy Quilt Bread, American Chapaties, Butter Crumb Rolls, Onion Rings, Swedish Tosca Coffee Cake, Swiss Fried Bread, and most of the supper and snack breads.

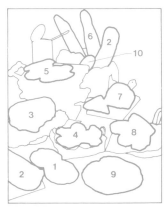

Breads Men Like to Bake:
1. Ranch-Style Cinnamon Rolls
2. Steak Sandwich Bread
3. Tailgater's Loaf
4. Doughnut Chips
5. Coney Islands
6. French Baguettes
7. Dinner-in-a-Loaf
8. Blue Cheese Flip
9. Dansk Sandwich
10. Hero Buns

WHITE MOUNTAIN LOAF

This billowy white cloud-like loaf is full of all kinds of old-fashioned goodness.

BAKE: 375° F. for 30 to 35 minutes   MAKES: 1 loaf

1 loaf frozen white bread dough, partially thawed
(French bread dough works well, too)
soft or melted butter or margarine
flour

Brush top half of loaf generously with butter. Roll in flour to coat generously. Place on greased cookie sheet. Cover; let rise in warm place until very light or doubled in size. (A frozen loaf will take from 3 to 6 hours, depending on the rising temperature. See label for more information.)

Bake at 375° F. for 30 to 35 minutes.

DINNER-IN-A-LOAF

Man-sized buns that would be good for a sportsman.

BAKE: 325° F. for 45 minutes   MAKES: 2 large buns (4 to 6 servings)

1 loaf frozen white (or honey wheat) bread dough, thawed
1 pound lean ground beef
2 cups finely chopped potato and rutabaga
1 small onion, chopped
2 stalks celery, chopped
¼ cup catsup
1½ teaspoons salt
¼ teaspoon pepper
milk
seasoned salt

Let dough rise until doubled in size. Combine remaining ingredients. Divide dough in half and roll out each half on floured surface to a 12-inch circle. Top half of each circle with half the filling. Fold in half; moisten and seal edges. Prick tops. Brush with milk and sprinkle with seasoned salt. Cover; let rise in warm place 30 minutes.

Bake at 325° F. for 45 minutes. Serve warm or cold. If served cold, keep refrigerated or in a cooler and use within a day.

DANSK SANDWICHES

Intriguing large open-faced sandwiches. You can experiment with some of your own topping ideas.

Lebanese Bread, page 25
Fresh chopped vegetables—cucumber, green pepper, onion, tomato, celery
shredded Cheddar or pizza cheese
seasoned salt

Slice bread horizontally. Butter and top with a combination of the suggested chopped vegetables. Sprinkle with seasoned salt; then generously top with cheese. Broil until cheese is melted and bubbly. Serve immediately.

BEEF-EATER'S SPECIAL:
Top each slice of bread with crumbled lean *ground beef,* finely chopped *onion* and *seasoned salt,* covering completely. Broil 5 to 8 minutes; then sprinkle with *cheese* and broil until melted and bubbly.

STEAK SANDWICH BREAD

A less expensive steak dinner; add a tossed salad and a vegetable and you will have a deluxe meal with not much work.

BAKE: 400° F. for 20 to 25 minutes   MAKES: 2 sandwich loaves
                                                    (8 to 10 servings)

1 loaf frozen white (French or honey wheat) bread dough, thawed
butter
flour
seasoned salt
2 to 3 pounds top round steak, cut 2 inches thick
¼ cup Italian dressing
1 tablespoon soy sauce
salt and pepper

Let dough rise slightly. Divide in half. Press out each half to 10x4-inch rectangle. Brush tops generously with soft butter or margarine. Coat generously with flour and sprinkle with seasoned or plain salt. Place on greased cookie sheet. Cover; let rise in warm place until light or doubled in size, 1 to 1½ hours.

Bake at 400° F. for 20 to 25 minutes.

Place meat in shallow dish. Pour dressing and soy sauce over meat. Refrigerate and let marinate several hours or overnight. For medium rare steak broil or grill over hot charcoal 30 minutes (15 minutes on each side). To serve, cut across the grain into very thin slices. Cut loaves in half horizontally. Butter lightly and fill with meat. If desired, heat meat juice and spoon over meat. Salt and pepper to taste.

TIP: For 4 or 5 servings, freeze one of the baked loaves for another time.

CONEY ISLANDS

These grilled frankfurters, topped with hot baked beans, are an old favorite.

BAKE: 400° F. for 15 to 20 minutes   MAKES: 6 or 8 servings

1 loaf frozen white (or honey wheat) bread dough, thawed
1 can (15 oz.) baked beans
6 or 8 frankfurters
seasoned salt

Divide dough into 6 or 8 pieces. Shape each into oblong bun about 5 inches long. Place on greased cookie sheet. Sprinkle with seasoned salt. Cover; let rise in warm place until light or doubled in size, 1 to 1½ hours.

Bake at 400° F. for 15 to 20 minutes. To serve, split each bun and fill with a grilled frankfurter and hot baked beans.

OATMEAL WHEAT ROLLS

These wheat rolls coated all the way around with oatmeal make a great conversation piece.

BAKE: 375° F. for 12 to 15 minutes   MAKES: 12 large buns

1 loaf frozen honey wheat (or white) bread dough, thawed
milk
rolled oats

Divide dough into 12 pieces. Shape each into ball. Brush lightly all the way around with milk. Roll in oats; place in well-greased muffin cups. Cover; let rise in warm place until light or doubled in size, 1½ to 2 hours.

Bake at 375° F. for 12 to 15 minutes.

OATMEAL HAMBURGER WHEAT BUNS:
Place shaped rolls 3 inches apart on greased cookie sheet; flatten slightly. Let rise and bake.

DOUGHNUT CHIPS

So easy—snip the dough into small pieces, let it rise, and fry it for a doughnut treat.

DEEP FAT FRY: 365° F. for 2 to 3 minutes   MAKES: 24 chips

1 loaf frozen white (or sweet) bread dough, thawed

Divide or cut dough into 24 pieces. Place 2 inches apart on floured cookie sheets. Cover; let rise in warm place until light or doubled in size, 1 to 1½ hours.

Fry in deep hot fat (365° F.) 2 to 3 minutes, turning to brown on both sides. Place on absorbent paper. Roll in sugar or frost with one of the icings on page 118.

FRENCH APPLE COFFEE CAKE

A coffee cake covered with apples and the topping from French apple pie.

BAKE: 350° F. for 30 to 35 minutes   MAKES: 2 (13-inch) coffee cakes

1 loaf frozen white (or sweet) bread dough, thawed
4 cups chopped pared apples
¾ cup sugar
½ cup flour
1 teaspoon cinnamon
¼ cup butter or margarine

Let dough rise until doubled in size. Roll out half of dough on floured surface to a 13-inch circle. Place in greased pizza pan or on cookie sheet lined with foil and greased. Top with half the apples. Combine sugar with remaining ingredients until crumbly; sprinkle half over apples. Repeat with remaining dough. Cover; let rise in warm place 30 minutes.

Bake at 350° F. for 30 to 35 minutes, or until apples are tender. If desired, frost with Vanilla Icing, page 118. Best warm.

OATMEAL WHEAT BREAD

A special wheat bread with a crunchy oatmeal crust.

BAKE: 375° F. for 30 to 35 minutes   MAKES: 1 loaf

1 loaf frozen honey wheat dough
milk
rolled oats

Brush the loaf of frozen dough with milk (all the way around). Generously sprinkle with (or roll in) rolled oats. Place in well-greased bread loaf pan. Cover; let rise in warm place until doubled in size.

Bake at 375° F. for 30 to 35 minutes.

TAILGATER'S LOAF:
Bake Oatmeal Wheat Bread in a well-greased 1½-quart oval (for football) or round (for baseball) casserole. Cool completely and cut horizontally into 4 slices. Butter slices. Combine 1½ cups each: finely cubed *ham* or other meat and shredded Cheddar or pizza *cheese*. Sprinkle each slice with about 1 cup of mixture and restack the loaf. Wrap in foil and heat in 350° F. oven about 30 minutes. To serve, insert bamboo skewers vertically into loaf for each slice. Top each skewer with an olive or other relish piece. Cut vertically into slices.

FRENCH BAGUETTES

Long skinny loaves that resemble the bread so popular in France. The authentic way to eat the bread is to have each person break off a chunk of bread.

BAKE: 325° F. for 30 to 35 minutes   MAKES: 2 (16-inch) loaves

1 loaf frozen white (or French) bread dough, thawed
1 tablespoon beaten egg white or egg
1 tablespoon water

Let dough rise until almost doubled in size. Divide in half. Shape into 16-inch strips on lightly floured surface. Place on greased cookie sheet. Combine egg and water; brush over loaves. With sharp knife, make several cuts across top of loaf. Cover; let rise in warm place until very light or doubled in size, 45 to 60 minutes.

Bake at 325° F. for 30 to 35 minutes, or until rich golden brown.

RANCH-STYLE CINNAMON ROLLS

Giant-size cinnamon rolls that will satisfy a hungry man.

BAKE: 375° F. for 15 to 20 minutes   MAKES: 6 large rolls

1 loaf frozen white (or sweet) bread dough, thawed
3 tablespoons butter or margarine, melted
⅓ cup sugar
1 teaspoon cinnamon
¼ cup finely chopped nuts

Let dough rise until doubled in size. Roll out on floured surface to a 15x10-inch rectangle. Brush with most of the butter. Combine sugar, cinnamon, and nuts; sprinkle most over dough. Roll up, starting with 10-inch side. Cut into 6 pieces. Place 2 inches apart, on greased cookie sheet. Flatten to about ½ inch; brush with remaining butter and sprinkle with sugar mixture. Cover; let rise in warm place until light, 30 to 45 minutes.

Bake at 375° F. for 15 to 20 minutes. Frost warm rolls with a half-recipe of one of the icings on page 118.

BLUE CHEESE FLIP

A giant Parker House roll flipped over a blue cheese-flavored filling. Good with roast pork or chops.

BAKE: 375° F. for 25 to 30 minutes   MAKES: 1 loaf

1 loaf frozen white bread dough, thawed
2 tablespoons crumbled blue cheese
⅓ cup (3 oz.) cream cheese, room temperature
¼ cup finely chopped onion
1 tablespoon cream or milk
butter

Let dough rise slightly. Roll out on floured surface to a 14x9-inch rectangle. Combine remaining ingredients. Spread over dough ½ inch from edges. Fold in half lengthwise just so 14-inch edges meet. Place on greased cookie sheet. Brush with soft butter. Cover; let rise in warm place until light or doubled in size, 1 to 1½ hours.

Bake at 375° F. for 25 to 30 minutes. Delicious warm.

PATIO CHEESE SNACKS

Buttery rich cheese tidbits that make a great appetizer.

BAKE: 375° F. for 20 to 25 minutes   MAKES: 36 snacks

1 loaf frozen white bread dough, thawed
¼ cup butter or margarine
garlic salt
½ cup chopped ripe olives
1 cup shredded Cheddar cheese

Melt butter in 13x9-inch pan; butter sides. Divide dough into 36 small pieces; place in pan turning to coat all sides with butter. Cover; let rise in warm place until very light or doubled in size, 1 to 1½ hours. Sprinkle bread lightly with garlic salt, olives, and cheese.

Bake at 375° F. for 20 to 25 minutes, or until a golden brown. Loosen edges and turn out of pan. Best warm. (May be wrapped in foil and reheated.)

Appendix

RECIPES TO ENHANCE BREADS
ICINGS

VANILLA OR ALMOND ICING:

1 cup powdered sugar
1 tablespoon soft butter or margarine
½ teaspoon vanilla or almond extract
3 to 4 teaspoons milk

Combine all ingredients, mixing until smooth. For frosting warm breads, add milk until icing is of a spreading consistency. If breads are frosted cold, you will want to add more milk, to get a glaze that will run slightly down the sides.

ORANGE ICING: Substitute *orange juice* for milk and add 2 teaspoons grated *orange peel*

LEMON ICING: Substitute *lemon juice* for milk and add 1 teaspoon grated *lemon peel*

CINNAMON OR NUTMEG ICING: Add ½ teaspoon *cinnamon* or *nutmeg* to icing

COFFEE ICING: Dissolve ½ teaspoon instant coffee in 2 tablespoons hot *water;* substitute for milk. Or use hot perked coffee.

MAPLE ICING: Substitute *maple flavoring* for vanilla.

RUM ICING: Substitute *rum flavoring* for vanilla.

BROWNED BUTTER ICING:

2 tablespoons butter (not margarine)
1 cup powdered sugar
½ teaspoon vanilla
1 to 2 tablespoons milk

Brown butter in small saucepan. Stir in powdered sugar and vanilla. Add milk until of spreading consistency.

Appendix:
1. Orange Butter
2. Herb Butter
3. Brown Betty
4. Decoupage Bread Wreath
5. Bread Pudding
6. Bread Crumbs
7. Crouton Sticks
8. Crouton Chips
9. Apple Pudding
10. Rusks or Oven Toast
11. Cinnamon Sugar
12. Lemon Sauce

FLAVORED BUTTERS

Butter with a perked up flavor makes an interesting spread for breads. Use the fruit-flavored butters for coffee cake breads and the zippy spreads for dinner breads, rolls, and snack breads. Serve butters with breads, or butter breads before serving. Another idea is to butter the bread and then heat in foil or toast under the broiler or on a grill. The flavor melts into the breads.

½ cup butter or margarine, room temperature
pinch of salt

Place butter, salt, and one of the recommended seasonings below in a small mixing bowl. Cream or blend together.

LEMON: 2 teaspoons grated *lemon peel* and 2 teaspoons *lemon juice*

ORANGE: 1 tablespoon grated *orange peel* and I tablespoon *orange juice*

NUTMEG: ¼ teaspoon *nutmeg* and 1 teaspoon grated *orange peel*

GARLIC: 1 small clove *garlic*, crushed, or 1 teaspoon garlic powder

ANCHOVY: 2 teaspoons *anchovy paste* or 3 *anchovy fillets*, ½ teaspoon grated *lemon peel*, and 1 teaspoon prepared *horseradish*

BLUE CHEESE: ½ cup crumbled *blue cheese* or 2 tablespoons blue cheese salad topping and ¼ teaspoon *smoke sauce*, if desired

CHEESE: ½ cup soft sharp Cheddar *cheese* and a dash of *cayenne*

PARMESAN CHEESE: ¼ cup *Parmesan cheese*, 1 tablespoon minced *onion*, ½ teaspoon *Worcestershire sauce*, and 1 teaspoon minced *parsley*

HERB: ½ teaspoon each: *thyme, oregano, marjoram,* and *parsley* and 2 teaspoons minced *onion* (or use 2 teaspoons of your own combination of herbs)

PARSLEY, DILL, or CHIVE: 2 tablespoons minced *parsley, dill,* or *chives,* 2 teaspoons *lemon juice,* and ⅛ teaspoon *white pepper*

CAPER: 2 tablespoons *capers,* 1 teaspoon minced *onion,* and ½ teaspoon grated *lemon peel*

ONION: ¼ cup finely chopped *onion* (or 1 tablespoon grated)

EGG WASH

This is what bakers use to give bread a shiny crust. It is also used to hold sesame, poppy, and other seeds to the crust. The usual proportions are equal amounts of slightly beaten egg or egg white and water or milk. A little of the mixture goes a long way.

1 tablespoon slightly beaten egg or egg white
1 tablespoon water or milk

Combine the egg and water. Brush carefully over bread as directed in recipe. (For a shinier and crisper crust decrease water to 1 teaspoon.) Egg wash may be brushed on the dough after shaping. Some people like to brush the breads after they have risen; however, it must be done carefully with a soft brush so the risen product will not collapse.

FLAVORED SUGARS

These sugars are good to sprinkle on hot buttered toast for an after-school snack. Or use them any time something just a little sweet is desired.

CINNAMON SUGAR: Combine ½ cup *sugar* and 2 teaspoons *cinnamon*

NUTMEG SUGAR: Combine ½ cup *sugar* and ½ teaspoon *nutmeg* or *mace*

ORANGE SUGAR: Combine ½ cup *sugar* and 2 teaspoons grated *orange peel*

LEMON SUGAR: Combine ½ cup *sugar* and 1 teaspoon grated *lemon peel*

VANILLA SUGAR: Split a *vanilla bean* and scrape seeds into 2 cups powdered or granulated sugar. Place in jar with tight cover. Let stand at least 1 week before using. (The powdered sugar is good to dust on sweet rolls and coffee cakes.)

SUGAR STREUSEL: Cut 2 tablespoons *butter* or margarine into ½ cup *flour*, 2 tablespoons *sugar*, and ¼ teaspoon *nutmeg* or *cinnamon* until particles are fine.

GOOD TO THE LAST CRUMB

To keep food costs at a minimum, it's important not to throw away extra food or what we usually call leftovers. If you're now throwing away the last slice or two of bread or coffee cake, or a sweet roll that has become a little dry, don't! There are many ways to use leftover breads.

BREAD CRUMBS: Crumbs can be made from almost any kind of bread, including many of the richer sweet breads. Let the bread dry completely, and then use a rolling pin or a blender to make crumbs. Store in a tight container in the refrigerator. You'll find it handy to have bread crumbs on hand.

Use crumbs from sweet breads to make desserts such as bread pudding or apple pudding, or use them to sprinkle over puddings. Perhaps you will want to brown the crumbs in a small amount of butter and add some almonds or coconut.

Season other bread crumbs by browning in butter and adding a few herbs. Bread crumbs are good to sprinkle on casseroles, to coat meats, and to garnish creamed dishes and rarebits.

CROUTONS: Cut sliced bread into ½-inch cubes. Place in a single layer in a large pan or sheet. Dry in a 250° F. oven 1½ to 2 hours, or until a light golden brown. If desired, sprinkle with melted butter and herbs, seasoned salts, or Parmesan cheese the last half-hour of baking. Stir occasionally while drying and browning. Use as a snack, on top of casseroles, or in soup, salads, or vegetables.

SWEDISH RUSKS OR OVEN TOAST: Cut bread into ½-inch slices. Place in a single layer on a cookie sheet. Brown in a 250° F. oven about 1½ to 2 hours or until light golden brown and crisp or dry. Turn about every half-hour while drying or browning.

APPLE PUDDING

BAKE: 350° F. for 40 to 45 minutes   MAKES: 6 servings

4 cups sliced, pared apples
¼ cup sugar
½ teaspoon cinnamon
½ cup brown sugar
1 cup bread crumbs
2 tablespoons coconut
¼ cup butter or margarine, melted

Combine apples, sugar, and cinnamon in shallow 8-inch baking dish. Combine remaining ingredients; sprinkle over apples. Bake at 350° F. for 40 to 45 minutes, or until apples are tender. Serve warm with cream.

BREAD PUDDING

BAKE: 350° F. for 45 to 60 minutes   MAKES: 6 servings

1½ cups bread cubes or coarse crumbs
½ cup raisins
⅓ cup sugar
½ teaspoon cinnamon
½ teaspoon vanilla
¼ teaspoon salt
3 eggs, beaten
3 cups hot milk

Combine all ingredients in 1½- or 2-quart casserole, stirring together carefully. Set casserole in pan of hot water. Bake at 350° F. for 45 to 60 minutes, or until knife inserted halfway between center and edge comes out clean. Best warm.

APPLE BROWN BETTY

BAKE: 375° F. for 45 to 60 minutes   MAKES: 6 servings

4 cups chopped, pared apples
¾ cup packed brown sugar
½ cup raisins, if desired
1 teaspoon cinnamon
¼ teaspoon salt
¼ cup butter or margarine, melted
3 cups small bread cubes or coarse crumbs
⅓ cup water

Combine the first 5 ingredients in mixing bowl. Combine butter and bread cubes. Alternate apples and bread in 2-quart casserole, beginning with apples and ending with the bread. Pour water over all. Bake, covered, at 375° F. for 30 minutes. Uncover and bake 15 to 30 minutes, or until top is browned and apples are tender. Serve hot with cream or a lemon sauce.

NOTE: Other fruits such as rhubarb may be substituted for the apples. With rhubarb, substitute 1¼ cups granulated sugar for the brown sugar.

DECORATIVE DECOUPAGE BREAD WREATH

Looking for a homey wall hanging for your kitchen?—Try making this varnished bread wreath that starts with a loaf of frozen bread dough.

BAKE: 375° F. for 25 to 30 minutes   MAKES: 1 wreath (about 12 inches in
                                                                        diameter)

1 loaf frozen white bread dough, thawed

Let dough rise until doubled in size. Divide into thirds. Shape each into 24-inch strip on floured surface. Braid together, stretching strips while braiding to keep even and uniform in length. Place in ring on greased cookie sheet. Seal ends together. Cover; let rise in warm place until light or doubled in size, 30 to 60 minutes.

Bake at 375° F. for 25 to 30 minutes, or until a very nice rich golden brown. Let dry in a cool dry place for several days until very hard. Glue a ring from a pop or juice can on the back at the seam. Brush varnish on both sides of the wreath several times. Or spray the wreath with a clear acrylic. The finished wreath should have a very heavy clear sheen of varnish. When dry, place an attractive bow and sheaf of grain at the top. Fasten a wire or string to the ring and hang.

TIP: A perfect braid is made by starting in the center and braiding both ways.

SHORT CUT WREATH: Divide the dough in half and make 24- to 30-inch strips. Twist the strips together to make the wreath.

Index

BREAD LOAVES

Bacon-Cheese Swirl 24
Barbecue Beef Loaf 16
Blue Cheese Flip 117
Braided Bread 23
Bubble Dinner Bread 16
Bundt Bread 17
Butter Crumb Monkey Loaf .. 21
Butter Crust Vienna Bread 20
Butterflake Loaf 23
Can Bread 21
Caraway Snack Bread 28
Caraway Wheat Bread 25
Casserole Herb Bread 17
Checkered Loaf 27
Cheese Bubble Loaf 108
Cheese Nugget Bread 23
Cheese Swirl 24
Christmas Bread 26
Cinnamon Swirl Bread 24
Crazy Quilt Round 27
Date Nut Bread 29
Down-to-Earth Wheat Bread .. 29
French Baguettes 116
French Bread Toasts 16
French Herb Loaf 22
French-Like Bread 16
Golden Braid 86
Golden Crown 22
Half 'n Half Bread 27
Hearth Bread 15
Herb Loaf 22
Herb Swirl 24
Honey Bee Twist 20
Individual Loaves 24
Lebanese Bread 25
Luncheon Bubble Ring 100
Mix and Match Braids 27
Mix and Match Bread 27

Oatmeal Wheat Bread 115
Old-Fashioned Loaf 15
Onion Swirl 24
Orange Prune Bread 28
Orange Raisin Swirl 24
Orange Raisin Wheat Bread .. 27
Pan Bread 17
Parker House Loaf 18
Patchwork Bread 27
Peanut Butter Swirl 24
Raisin Bread 20
Scandinavian Wheat Bread 25
Skillet Bread 18
Snack Wheat Bread 28
Steak Sandwich Bread 113
Taos Indian Bread 95
Triple Treat Loaf 26
Wheat Chips 28
Wheat Germ Bread 29
White Mountain Loaf 112

DINNER ROLLS

Bacon Cheese Crescents 40
Bacon Rolls 36
Braids 32
Breadsticks 38
Brioche Rolls 39
Butter Crumb Rolls 33
Butter-Crust Rolls 33
Butterflake (Fan Tan) Rolls .. 32
Butter Twists 32
Cheese-Caraway Rolls 36
Cloverleaf Rolls 32
Crescents 32
Curlicues 32
Dinner Buns 31
Dinner Rolls 31
Double Cheese Pinwheels 36
Double-Quick Dinner Rolls ... 38

Double Twists   32
English Muffins   41
English Muffin Supper Ideas . .   41
Fan Tan Rolls   32
Finger Rolls   31
Frankfurter Buns   33
Garden Rolls   37
Garlic Rolls   36
Hamburger Buns   33
Hamburger Hearth Buns   40
Hero Buns   37
Herb Rolls   36
Honey Rolls   42
Hot Cross Buns   94
Knots   32
Lucky Cloverleafs   32
Miniature Dinner Rolls 109
Oatmeal Hamburger Wheat
     Buns 115
Oatmeal Wheat Rolls   114
Onion-Dill Rolls   36
Onion Rings   39
Orange-Anise Rolls   36
Pan Rolls   31
Parker House Rolls   32
Parmesan Dinner Rolls 107
Peanut Butter Rolls   42
Peanut Butter Secrets   42
Pinwheels   32
Posies   33
Shamrock Rolls   32
Smoky-Barbecue Rolls   36
Speedy Cloverleafs   32
Super-Hamburger Buns   33
Twin Rolls   32
Two-Tone Braided Rolls   34
Two-Tone Cloverleafs   34
Two-Tone Marble Rolls   34
Two-Tone Pinwheel Rolls   34
Two-Tone Twin Rolls   34
White Mountain Rolls   32

SWEET ROLLS

Apple Pastries   60
Bismarks   63

Butterfly Cinnamon Rolls   46
Butterscotch Nut Buns   44
Caramel Nut Rolls   51
Cherry Chip Cookie Rolls   60
Cherry Streusel Triangles   58
Cinnamon Buns   44
Cinnamon Daisies   48
Cinnamon Jelly Rolls   48
Cinnamon Palm Leaves   46
Cinnamon Roll Doughnuts   61
Cinnamon Snails   53
Cookie Buns   57
Danish Butter Crispies   49
Danish Coffee Rolls   54
Danish Curlicues   55
Danish "S" Rolls   54
Date Twists   56
Deluxe Kolackies   59
Double Sweet Twists   57
Doughnut Chips 114
Doughnut Knots   63
Elephant Ears   49
Figure Eights   53
Glazed Lemon Rolls   53
Golden Orange Curlicues   55
Grandma's Raisin Sugar Rolls . .   51
Honey Buns   51
Honey Wheat Rolls   52
Jam Whirls   61
Jelly Rolls   52
Lemon Cookie Buns   57
Lemon Dessert Rolls   62
Lemon Drops   59
Long Johns   63
Maple Nut Wheat Rolls   52
Meringue Crescents   62
Mincemeat Rolls   54
Mini-Orange Rolls   45
Mom's Cinnamon Rolls   45
Nutty Cookie Rolls   60
Old-Fashioned Kolackies   59
Open-faced Kolackies   59
Orange Buns   44
Orange Cookie Buns   57
Orange Sticky Rolls   50
Orange Sugar Crispies   49

Orange Twists 56
Peanut Butter Jelly Rolls 52
Raised Doughnuts 63
Ranch-Style Cinnamon Rolls . . 116
Streusel Nut Squares 55
Sugar Chip Twists 56
Sunday Best Rolls 50
Swedish Cinnamon Rolls 46
Swedish Tea Ring 96
Swedish Twists 63
Sweet Cloverleafs 49
Sweet Knots 53
Sweet Whirlups 53
Sweetheart Rolls 58
Swiss Fried Bread 95
Taffy Rolls 51
Tiny Cinnamon Rolls 45
Walnut Twists 56

COFFEE CAKES AND LOAVES

Apple Kuchen 74
Apple Twirl 79
Apricot Baba Dessert 81
Apricot Blossom 81
Apricot Kuchen 74
Blueberry Flip 78
Blueberry Kuchen 74
Butterscotch Bubble Loaf 78
Butterscotch Coffee Cake 83
Butterscotch Crown 70
Butterscotch Nut Loaf 72
Butterscotch Snowballs 72
Cherry Pie Coffee Cake 79
Cherry Streusel 76
Christmas Crown 70
Christmas Tree 66
Cinnamon Logs or Crescents . . 66
Cinnamon Rings 66
Cinnamon Roll Coffee Cakes . . 66
Cinnamon Roll Loaf 68
Cinnamon Swirl Braid 69
Coconut Swirl 82
Cupid's Coffee Cake 67
Danish Caramel Coffee Cake . . 75
Danish Cream Coffee Cake 76

Deluxe Cinnamon Round 68
Dutch Sugar Cake 75
Easter Breakfast Coffee Cake . . 84
Easter Rabbit Coffee Cake 83
Easy Danish Kuchen 71
French Apple Coffee Cake 115
Frosty Snowball Cakes 73
Hawaiian Ring 80
Jelly Splits 82
Mock Almond Rolls 80
Mock Almond Twist 80
Monkey Bread 69
Moravian Coffee Cake 85
Orange Almond Coffee Cake
    Bars 77
Orange Coconut Bubble Loaf . . 69
Orange Twist Coffee Cake 71
Orange Streusel Coffee Cake . . 75
Peach Kuchen 74
Pineapple Upside Down Cake . . 84
Plum Kuchen 74
Potica (Polish Holiday Bread) 88
Quickie Orange Coffee Cake . . . 74
Raspberry Kuchen 74
Rhubarb Kuchen 74
Split Twirl Loaf 73
Streusel Coffee Cake 75
Swedish Church Bread 77
Swedish Cinnamon Coffee Cake 75
Swedish Tea Log 67
Swedish Tea Ring 96
Swedish Tosca Coffee Cake . . . 76
Sweet Braid 70

ETHNIC BREADS

American Chapaties 93
Cottage Cheese Potica 88
Danish Kringle 92
Danish Pastries 92
Golden Braid 86
Grecian Feast Bread 91
Hot Cross Buns 94
Houska 93
Italian Easter Egg Bread 94
Julekake 87

Kougelhof 91
Kulich 90
Lebanese Bread 25
Moravian Coffee Cake 85
Peda 95
Polish Babka 90
Poppy Seed Potica 88
Potica (Polish Holiday Bread) .. 88
Potica Fillings 88
Sally Lunn 87
Stollen 86
Swedish Tea Ring 96
Swedish Tea Ring Fillings 96
Swiss Fried Bread 95
Taos Indian Bread 95
Walnut Potica 88

SUPPER AND SNACK BREADS
A la King Sauce 41
American Chapaties 93
Skillet Beef-Burger 104
Barbecue Beef Loaf 16
Beef Bake 103
Beef-Eaters' Special 113
Beef Pasties 102
Bite-Sized Stuffies 105
Bologna Cheese Quickies 41
Cheese Bacon Snack Bread ...107
Cheese Bubble Loaf 108
Cheese Rarebit 41
Cheese Snack Bread 107
Chicken Sandwiches 101
Chip Dip 109
Chopped Beef Sandwiches 101
Cocktail Meatballs 109
Coney Islands 114
Corned Beef Sandwiches 101
Dansk Sandwiches 113
Dinner-in-a-Loaf 112
English Muffin Supper Ideas .. 41
French Snack Bread 107

Ground Beef Flip 98
Ham and Cheese Sandwiches ..101
Ham Flip 98
Ham Sandwiches 101
Ham-Stuffed Rolls 105
Hamburger-Stuffed Rolls 105
Luncheon Bubble Ring 100
Miniature Bow Knots 109
Miniature Dinner Rolls 109
Onion Kuchen 103
Onion Toppers 104
Onion Snack Bread 107
Parmesan Dinner Rolls 107
Patio Cheese Snacks 117
Peda 95
Pizza 106
Pizza, Deep Dish 97
Pizza Party 106
Pizza Toppings 106
Pigs-in-Blankets 100
Roast Beef Sandwiches 101
Roast Pork Sandwiches 101
Salami Sandwiches 101
Shrimp Salad 100
Skillet Beef-Burger 104
Skillet Turkey-Burger 104
Snack Sticks 109
Snack Wheat Bread 28
Stuffed Parmesan Rolls 107
Super Sandwiches 101
Tailgaters' Loaf 115
Tuna-Cheese Sandwiches 101
Tuna-Cheese Toppers 41
Tuna Cocktail Twirls 108
Tuna Flip 98
Turkey-Stuffed Rolls 105
Turkey Flip 98
Turkey Pasties 102
Turkey Sandwiches 101
Western Barbecue Beef 100
Wheat Chips 28

THE AUTHOR

Sylvia Ogren is recognized nation-wide as an outstanding authority on bread baking. A home economics consultant, she has worked for many major food companies including the Pillsbury Company, where she supervised much of the work behind the Pillsbury Bake-Off Contest.

Ms. Ogren earned a Bachelor's and a Master's degree in Home Economics at the University of Minnesota. She has written newspaper columns, developed thousands of recipes for cookbooks and recipe leaflets, supervised publication of the Pillsbury Bake-Off cookbooks, and helped to compile the original Pillsbury Family Cookbook.

In *Bake Breads from Frozen Dough* Ms. Ogren combines her creative ability with the practicality of frozen yeast doughs, to produce a unique set of tested, easy and delicious recipes.

Order **Bake Breads from Frozen Dough** from your bookstore, or send check for $6.95 direct to

DILLON PRESS, INC.
500 South Third Street
Minneapolis, Minnesota 55415